THE POSITIVE SIDE OF WHAT NO ONE KNOWS

The Positive Side of What No One Knows

Turning A Tragic Past Into A Positive Future

Stacy Lupinacci

© 2009 by Stacy Lupinacci All Rights Reserved

ISBN # 978-0-692-15322-2

*Note – I (the author) of this book is in NO way trying to administer ANY medical, legal, mental, or physical advice. If you believe you are being abused in any way, please contact your local law enforcement agency and your local crisis centers or shelters. You can find them in the blue pages of your local phone book. **If you are in immediate danger, please find the nearest phone and dial 911**

This book is dedicated to all of the survivors in the world.

May you always know how special you really are and that you have more strength and courage then you realize. Use that strength to overcome all of life's challenges. Make the most positive impact on humanity as possible. You have the power to change the world.

A special dedication goes out to my mother for finding the courage to leave her emotional and physically abusive relationship. She is an inspiration to many. Especially me. I love you Ma!!

"Controllers, abusers, and manipulative people don't ask themselves if the problem is them. They always say the problem is someone else."

~ Darlene Ouimet

Contents

Introduction

Chapter 1: Different Forms of Abuse
Chapter 2: Everyone Is At Risk
Chapter 3: The After School Gang
Chapter 4: The Monster In The Hallway
Chapter 5: Two Pathways To Abuse
Chapter 6: The Unknown Sibling
Chapter 7: Who Was He
Chapter 8: It Isn't Always Sexual Abuse
Chapter 9: You Are Not Alone
Chapter 10: Samantha's Story

Chapter 11: Edward's Story

Chapter 12: Donatello's Story

Chapter 13: Briana's Story

Chapter 14: How Your Loved Ones Cope

Chapter 15: Positive and Spiritual Recovery

Chapter 16: Not All Abusers Are Men

Chapter 17: A Note To Abusers

Resources

Introduction

For many years I sat back and watched how the world coped with abuse. As I thought about writing this book, I wondered how my stories could help those in need. Those that were in the same situation that I had been in or even experiencing now. What I mean by need is that when we as victims go through events such as abuse, we sometimes need help finding our true selves. That wonderful soul that we really are. Know that you are wonderful and deserve nothing but the absolute best in everything you do and everything you are.

Abuse isn't something new. It has been happening for thousands of years. We sometimes don't want to deal with it, but even if you don't "see" it, know that it is happening everywhere. You can take the positive side of life and turn any negative situation into a positive outcome in your life.

Some would ask," How can there be a positive side to abuse of any kind?" In the following pages, I will describe how what seems to be unforgivable acts of abuse and violence against someone can have a positive outcome in your life.

You might not want to talk about what happened to you but please do understand that reporting the abuse is a way to help others not become a victim of the abuser. It will also help you heal from your tragic assault and be able to see that it is <u>never</u> your fault and you deserve to be happy and live a very positive life.

Although exact ages are not always mentioned, I want to express that the events in my personal stories have occurred from the age of 5 years old to 10 years old unless otherwise noted.

I wanted to write this book to help others who may be going through some of the same experiences and let them now that they are not alone. You are a bright light in a sometimes dark world.

~ Enjoy~

Stacy Lupinacci

This affirmation comes from another bright light in this world. I feel it speaks to everyone everywhere. Know that you deserve the best of everything. You are beautiful and gorgeous and it is important to forgive. Don't ever allow anyone to make you feel different. I hope you enjoy.

" I am who I am. Appreciate me for me. We all make mistakes or you would not be human. No one is perfect. Thank God there is always room in this world for growth. Continue being who you are, which is a beautiful soul that will continue to shine. Light xoxoox."

~ Jill Dahne

"They say beauty is in the eye of the beholder, but who beholds the beauty in you?"

~ Stacy Lupinacci

CHAPTER 1

Different Forms of Abuse

Emotional Abuse

Emotional Abuse – Emotional abuse is when verbal, physical, or threats of abuse affects you mentally and brings you spiritually down often lowering your self-esteem. It is similar to brainwashing.

Emotional abuse and physical abuse for the most part go hand in hand. There are millions of cases where physical abuse stems from months even years of emotional abuse. After the physical abuse starts, the emotional abuse has most likely already been in existence.

In most stories that I have heard from people, the emotional abuse started before the physical abuse. There are people out in the world that have gone through a lot of emotional abuse themselves, which can (not necessarily set in stone that they will) lead to them being abusers and/or victims of abuse. Now this isn't the case in every situation

Due to the lack of emotional abuse cases being reported it is hard to get accurate statistics. Do know that this occurs far more then anyone can even imagine.

- Your partner swears and/or yells at you.
- Your partner repeatedly harasses, interrogates you, or degrades you.
- Your partner uses name calling, put-downs and ridicules against you.
- Your partner insults the people you care for, your family and friends.
- Your partner threatens to harm you or your family.
- Your partner controls and/or limits your behavior by keeping you from using the phone or seeing friends, not letting you leave the room or the house, following you and monitoring or limiting your phone conversations.
- Your partner forces you to stay awake or repeatedly wakes you from sleep.
- Your partner blames you for the way he/she treats you.
- Your partner forces you to do degrading things, such as making you kneel or making you beg for money.

- Your partner criticizes your thoughts, feelings, opinions, beliefs, and actions.
- Your partner is extremely jealous, constantly accusing you of flirting or cheating.
- Your partner tells you that you are "sick" or "crazy"

(www.healthline.com)

- Does your partner embarrass you in front of your friends and family?
- Does your partner threaten you with a weapon?
- Does your partner make you feel like you can't make your own decisions?
- Does your partner threaten to harm your pets?

This is only a small list of symptoms that emotional abuse victims go through. If you are experiencing one or more of the above statements, you are being extremely abused and should seek help immediately.

All of these and more can hurt you spiritually also. I'm not talking about religion. I'm talking about the core of your essence. The real you. When you are a victim of abuse, whether it is, physical, sexual, emotional or spiritual, you start to operate on a lower vibrational level. You lose your confidence in yourself. You lose respect for yourself and your self-worth. Remember you are worthy of being loved in the loving positive way a person should be. You don't deserve to be treated any other way.

Examples of someone having and emotional hold on you after the relationship, include, but not limited to:

- Trust Issues
- Physically detaching from friends and family.
- Emotional detachment
- Having the need to control future relationships

Some of the comments an abuser uses towards their victims include, but not limited to:

- "No one will ever love you like me!"
- "You'll never find someone like me!"
- "Look at you, who else besides me will ever love or want you!"

Let me comment to those statements by saying,

"I SURE HOPE NOT!!" AND "RUN!!!"

You deserve to be treated like the wonderful person that you are. Let your inner light pave the way through a sometimes dark world. Sometimes, we don't see the rainbow because it is blocked by the tunnel we have to go through to get to the end. There is a pot of gold at the end of the rainbow. It's called happiness. Go for it! You deserve it!

Rape / Sexual Assault

To get the exact definition of rape or sexual assault, you have to check within your own state as some states can use different wording tactics to mean the same thing. I am going to express the definition as it stands in certain states that use these terms separately. Please check your local rape crisis center or police for the exact terminology that your state uses.

<u>Rape</u> – Any forced sexual intercourse, including vaginal, anal, or oral penetration. Penetration may be by a body part or any foreign object.

<u>Sexual Assault</u> – Any unwanted sexual contact that stops short of penetration. This also includes unwanted touching and fondling. (Please remember that some states use this term to include penetration and <u>any</u> form of unwanted sexual contact.)

I want to mention that unwanted sexual contact with another adult isn't the only form of sexual abuse. If the victim involved is under the legal age to have consensual sex in that particular state, even if they say yes, it is still legally not allowed. Rape/sexual assault is for the majority of the cases performed by someone that the victim knows personally. Although there are numerous reports from victims that did not know their assailant, in most cases this is the case.

Sexual Assault is not something that someone does because they love you or want to be with someone sexually. This act of violence is due to the abuser's desire for control and to express their power. Remember that even though you don't say no for the fear of something worse happening to you, it is still considered assault. It is important for you to keep yourself safe.

Rape/sexual assault happens to everyone in every race, gender, sexual orientation, religious background, education, and social economic background. No one is exempt from this act of violence reaching and possibly happening to you and/or someone you know.

A leading misconception is that if you are a married couple, you are entitled sex from your partner. The truth is, this is far from the truth. No one is entitled to have sex with you, nor do they have the right just because of their relationship with you. No is no, no matter how you know that person.

SEXUAL ABUSE and CHILDREN

Sexual abuse in children in my opinion, is one of the most reprehensible things you can do to a child. There is absolutely no excuse for it. That is my human feelings on this topic.

Once again, depending on what state you live in, laws regarding what is considered child sexual assault and incest as they vary from state to state. I myself see a difference in the two and so for the sake of argument, I will give what I believe as well as some states to be the difference.

<u>Incest</u> – unwanted sexual contact between people who are closely related. (ie-parent/child, uncles/aunts, siblings, cousins, niece/nephew)

<u>Child Sexual Assault</u> – unwanted sexual contact to a child by someone of significant age and/or size difference.

Incest

I believe the difference is that although both can do a lot of damage to a child mentally, physically, emotionally, and spiritually. When a child is experiencing incest is it is in my opinion, worse because it is by someone the child is supposed to look to for support. It is someone who is supposed to be the one they go to for everything including safety.

Most children who experience incest might never say anything for a number of reasons. These reasons may include but not limited to:

- They are told, "It's normal. Everyone is doing it. All families are like this.
- The victim is afraid of retaliation.
- The victim doesn't feel safe telling anyone due to the lack of security.
- No one will believe them.

Please know that if you are currently a victim of incest or that you have been a victim, it is NEVER your fault. No matter what anyone says, YOU DID NOTHING WRONG.

Child Sexual Assault

Much like incest, sexual assault on a child by anyone can be very damaging to a child's well being. Most of the time the abuse is by someone known to the child, but not a close relative.

The following is a list of warning signs that your child may be a victim of sexual abuse (these are just a few common signs. It doesn't mean that it is guaranteed that your child is being abused. Please contact your family physician for advice on your individual case.)

- Difficulty walking or sitting
- Bloody, torn, or stained underclothes
- Bleeding, bruises, or swelling in the genital area
- Sexually Transmitted Infections, especially if the child is under 14 years old
- Says they have been abused
- Inappropriate sexual knowledge and behavior
- Withdrawal
- School Problems
- Anxiety
- Guilt

(www.rainn.org – This is just a short list.)

The Rainn, Abuse and Incest National Network is an absolutely wonderful organization with a very resourceful website for education and can help you find help if you have been or currently being abused.

Please note that no matter what you are told, you never deserved this. It is morally and legally wrong and you are entitled to safe and professional help. Please tell a teacher, a school counselor, a friend, another relative or a friend's parent. Never believe this is your fault. It never is!

Domestic Violence

Domestic Violence (DV) - is described as a pattern of behavior in any relationship that is used to gain or maintain power and control over an intimate partner.

(www.ndvh.org)

Many people including women AND men are victims of domestic violence everyday. Domestic Violence is not prejudice against any gender, socioeconomic status, age, racial, or sexual orientation group. You can be married, living together or just dating. It doesn't matter. It can happen to you.

- Does your partner intimidate you?
- Do they make threats of harming you , your pets, or themselves?
- Does your partner call you names and constantly out you down?
- Does your partner physically assault you?
- Does your partner try to control everything you say or do?
- Does your partner try and keep you from your family?
- Does your partner use finances against you or make you beg for money?
- Does your partner tell you that if you behaved, they wouldn't get so mad?

If you answered yes to any of these questions, you are a victim of domestic violence. You need to remove yourself from the situation as soon as possible. You might think it is hard and often it is but it is much better for everyone involved for you to NOT be there.

I, myself was in an abusive relationship once. I vowed never again. I didn't stay long enough to let the physical abuse get any worse. The emotional abuse happened often but I felt trapped so I stayed but once it got physical, I knew I had to leave.

My mother was in abusive relationships until she finally got the courage to leave. Her last abusive relationship took her 7 years to leave. It didn't have to last that long but looking at her relationship, I refused to let that be me, and it hasn't.

I have heard it said that physical abuse isn't so bad because once the bruises are gone, that's it. That is not true at all. With every hit you endure, you are also being knocked down emotionally and spiritually. You deserve to live your life abuse free. You are better than what you are going through.

Everyone knows someone who has been or who is currently being physically abused. Much of the time, the victims are good at hiding what is really happening to them. Just because you see a couple in public and they are smiling and look like they are enjoying life,doesn't mean everything is ok. A great movie that not only is super funny but also pertains to domestic violence in what is looked to be higher class society is, Tyler Perry's Madea's Family Reunion. It is a great movie with a wonderful story line. I highly recommend it to anyone.

- Every day three women are murdered by their intimate partners.
- 61 percent of women murdered by males were killed by husbands or male partners.
- 20 percent of teenage girls and young women have experienced some form of dating violence.
- Half of men who abuse their wives also abuse their children.
- When an intimate partner inflicted an injury upon a woman, she reported the violence to the police only 55% of the time.
- Up to 13 million children a year witness domestic violence.
- Every year, almost 6% of California's women suffer physical injuries from domestic violence.
- Abuse in relationships exists among all classes, races and cultural groups, although women between ages 16 and 24 are nearly three times more vulnerable to intimate partner violence.
- Domestic violence in the United States costs an estimated $67 billion annually.

(www.standagainstdv.org)

The ego and the self dwell in the same body- The former eats the sweet and sour fruits of the tree of life, while the latter looks on in detachment

~ Unknown

~~~~~~~~~~~

Victims continue to live in the past. Survivors live in the now and strive for the future

~~~~~~~~~~~

CHAPTER 2

Everyone Is At Risk

Women as Victims

Women for years have been stereotyped as the weaker gender. Now although this is not true, when a woman has been assaulted, she sometimes question if in fact it is considered rape/sexual assault. Some of these concerns include but limited to ;

- If I didn't fight then I must have wanted it. Is it still rape/sexual assault?
- Well one of us were drinking. So if it happened, is it still wrong?
- We are married, so isn't it my duty to have sex with my partner even if I don't want to?

These are common and valid concerns and answers that many victims have. I am going to respond to these by saying;

- Just saying NO is enough for them to stop. Anything after that is assault.
- Both participants must have a clear mental, and conscious ability to consent. Anything else is unacceptable.
- It is no one's "duty" to have sex with another person just because you are married to them. (Please check with your local rape crisis center and/or local police as different states have different laws pertaining to that particular state.)
- At least one in every three women has been beaten, coerced into sex or otherwise abused during her lifetime.
- 13% of college women indicated that they had been forced to have sex in a dating situation
- Approximately one in five high school students reports being physically and/or sexually abused by a dating partner.
- Between 25% and 33% of same sex couples experience battering behavior.
- Of the estimated more than 1 million persons age 65 and over who are victims of abuse each year. At least two-thirds are women.

(www.loveisnotabuse.com)

Women have been told over the years that they need to obey what their partners say. This includes sex. This is simply not true. You own your own body. You have the right to say if you want to have sex with someone. No one holds that power over you. A lot of women are raised to believe this as well. This is also simply not true.

Over the years, from many outlets, we are taught that we have to be subservient to "men". Women believe that what a man says, goes. We as women also have grown up to believe that when a man gets mad and abuses us, emotionally and/or physically, we must have deserved it. The truth is, no one deserves to be abused. No woman deserves to have a man or anyone raise a hand to her, emotionally tear her down, or force oneself on another.

Don't let your abuser take your soul per se. Live your life being understanding and loving. Sometimes, our abusers are allowed to have that hold on us. We take our anger and our hurt and confusion out on the wrong people. I can't say it enough, "Don't let negative past, affect your positive future." Let yourself be the wonderful person you are!

- **One in every four women** will experience domestic violence in her lifetime.
- An estimated 1.3 million women are victims of physical assault by an intimate partner each year.
- 85% of domestic violence victims are women.
- Historically, females have been most often victimized by someone they knew.
- Females who are **20-24 years of age** are at the greatest risk of nonfatal intimate partner violence
- Most cases of domestic violence are never reported to the police.
- Almost **one-third of female homicide victims** that are reported in police records are killed by an intimate partner.
- In 70-80% of intimate partner homicides, no matter which partner was killed, the man physically abused the woman before the murder.
- Approximately one-half of the orders obtained by women against intimate partners who physically assaulted them were violated. More than two-thirds of the restraining orders against intimate partners who raped or stalked the victim were violated.

(www.ncadv.org)

Knowledgeable resources are out there to assist you in finding help. It may be hard to do, but it can be done. Don't let yourself become a statistic.

Men as Victims

Men are victims too!

Sometimes, you hear people say there is no way a man can be the victim of abuse, but know that it can and does happen. In a later chapter, hear from a woman that abused as well as being abused.

Men have a vulnerable side to them but more often than not, they don't show that side of them for fear of what others may think (namely society). Whether they want to admit it or not, they do cry. This is actually a good thing. It shows that they are human beings with feelings also. This in no way makes them less than a man, but shows more of a spiritual being having a human experience.

Men are said to be the solid rocks of the world, but as that may be, there are times when even the biggest boulders have their weak point. This allows them to break down and open, showing their inner and true selves.

They don't want other people to see them and they think they are not manly enough. Trust me! A man that can be rough and tough but still show his true feelings in a gentle way, to me, is more of a real man than those that play the tough guy that puts everyone down because he is afraid of what others will say about him.

Now, I'm not saying this because I want you to think that all men are putting up a wall and have some big secret to hide, but men that have been a witness or a victim to abuse can put up that macho tough guy attitude as a way of covering up what they feel and what they have been through.

Are you a guy that has witnessed abuse or have been abused and you think it hasn't affected you? Yes it has. It is ok to admit it. There are millions of men out there in similar situations as you. You are not alone!

When you witness someone being abused, ie your mom, your father, a sibling, a close friend; that affects you. It affects your way of thinking and your mental state. It can and will affect your perception on how the world works. Both good and bad. When you witness abuse in the home, that is a form of emotional abuse. This has led to millions of men to be in a relationship where they themselves are the victim and/or the abuser. Know that you deserve better then either of these lifestyles.

Maybe you grew up in a loving and caring home, but for some reason you tend to attract a partner who is abusive. This may be because you are not secure in yourself. Maybe you have low self-esteem because you were picked on as a child for being overweight or even too skinny. Maybe you had acne when you were a teenager and felt ugly because of things people said to you. This could all lead to low self-esteem issues and open you up to attract people who show you attention, but it might not be the right attention. Sometimes it could also lead you abuse others to make you feel good about yourself. This still makes you a victim but it could also makes you the abuser.

I don't care if you are 200 pounds overweight, 100 pounds underweight, or have acne so bad that it looks like you have road rash on your face. You deserve to be happy and treated with respect. You deserve to be loved by someone who cares about the beautiful you inside.

Never let anyone make you feel less than the important man that you are. No one deserves to be ridiculed, made fun of, told you are not worthy of finding better, hit you, have things thrown at, or even forced to have sex if you don't want to. Yes, men can be forced to have sex, just as much as women.

These are a few concerns that male victims have but in no way are they the only concerns.

- I'm a guy and I got aroused during the course of the action. I must have wanted it.
- I'm a man and she is the woman. It's not assault if she wants sex and I don't.
- I didn't want to have sexual contact with them, but because we are in a same sex relationship, it isn't rape/sexual assault.

These are very valid concerns and here is my response to them:

- Being aroused is a natural and physical response that is sometimes actually out of your control. If you didn't want the sexual advances of the other person, then that constitutes assault.
- To have consensual sex is that it must be agreed upon by both participants. Anything more is illegal.
- That is not true. <u>Any</u> unwanted sexual advances, no matter what your sexual

preference is, is illegal and should be reported.

Any way you look at it, you have the same rights as any one else when it comes to being abused. You have the right to seek help and leave the situation. There are numerous resources to help you find the help you need to build your self-esteem so that you see your self worth. Please check with your local rape crisis center and/or law enforcement agency for exact laws in your state.

Children as Victims

There are numerous forms of child abuse. Children are the leaders of this world , and I personally hate to look at photos where a child has been abused. It just breaks my heart to stand witness to a child who is helpless and defenseless, have to endure the cruel torture this world has to dish out.

For many years children have had to deal with physical, emotional, and even sexual abuse. These are the events I believe we all go through to help us learn from. I can not for the life of me, wrap my emotional or intellectual matter to accept it. Young children are very impressionable and being put in a situation like this, is emotionally disturbing.

According to www.loveisnotabuse.com, in the year 2000, an estimated 1200 children died of abuse and neglect, which narrows down to an average of 3 children a day. One per day it too much so three per day is too much for any country in this world. We need to put a stop to this now! Not when this hit close to our personal homes. Let's prevent this from getting to your personal home.

We all face economic hardships. Many young children are being left home alone for long hours while a parent works to make ends meet for the home. Parents are losing sight of parenthood by losing their tempers and physically abusing their children. This is never acceptable no matter what the situation is.

Child abuse is described as any action that endangers a child's physical or mental health. Some of the warning signs that a child may be abused or neglected includes but not limited to:

- Nervousness around adults
- Aggression towards adults or children
- Sudden or dramatic changes in personality or activities
- Acting out sexually or showing interest in sex that is not appropriate for his or her age

- Frequent or unexplained bruises or injuries
- Low self-esteem
- Poor Hygiene

www.loveisnotabuse.com

I recommend everyone listen to a song by Martina McBryde called, Concrete Angel. If you have computer access, please go to Youtube and type in this URL: http://www.youtube.com/watchv=KtNYA4pAGjI That will take you to Martina's channel and you can see her video. It goes along with the song and it will give you an idea of what children go through and we may never even know. It's a beautiful song that speaks the truth about our children and what abuse can do to them.

As a community, we need to come together and help raise these children and protect them. There is an old saying, "It takes a village to raise a child." We get so wrapped up in our lives, that we don't want to seem nosy, or interfere with the way someone raises their children, but the truth is, it's our responsibility to protect the innocent, including the innocent children of the world. They can't defend themselves when it comes to the physical abuse of an adult.

Sometimes, an adult is stuck in a pattern of abuse when it comes to raising children as they were abused as children themselves. Maybe their own parents had short tempers and therefore became physically abusive to them as well. This does not in any way, condone what they are doing, but we as a community can help their parents also.

As I mentioned earlier in the chapter, neglect of a child is also a form of abuse. Maybe you live next door to a single parent who always seems to be at work. Maybe their home isn't the cleanest because they are always working a double shift, and by the time they get home, cleaning is the last thing on their mind.

Instead of judging these parents as we all as humans do, try offering to help them. Offer to come over and help clean up their home. If you have a few dollars to spare, go to your local goodwill, salvation army, or thrift store and get a nice outfit for their child for about $7.00. Maybe you have a child who has outgrown their clothes and they are in good condition, offer them to your neighbor. If their clothes are always dirty, offer to help them with their laundry. You can lend a hand and offer to babysit for a couple of hours so the parent (s) can go out for a few hours. Ask a neighbor over for dinner to take the burden off them rushing home to cook.

Please don't be mistaken that the hard working, middle class families are the only ones in this situation. Upper class also has abuse in their families. If you have witnessed excessive yelling and children are crying more then usual, please do not turn your tv up to avoid hearing the "loud noises". Call your local Social Services or Child Protective Services (CPS) and 911. You could be saving a life.

Abuse in Same Sex Relationships

You don't have to be in a heterosexual relationship for it to be an abusive relationship. Same sex relationships are also capable of being abusive. Know that is not ok for anyone to abuse you and you are <u>never</u> alone, <u>ever</u>! Domestic Violence, including, sexual and emotional abuse does not discriminate any race, gender, economic status, or sexual orientation.

Same sex relationships are not excluded from the abuse world. They have the same problems that everyone has. You, or you relationship is no different than anyone else in this world. Ok, so maybe the difference is that there are two people of the same gender in the relationship, but who's to say that is not normal? Who's to say that in today's day and age, heterosexual relationships aren't considered abnormal. Who's to say they were ever the "normal" ones. Everyone is a human being and should be treated as such.

Yes there are still people that think same sex relationships are wrong, but if you look at the way they themselves think of the world, a lot of what they deem appropriate, may not be. They are all entitled to their opinions, but don't let their opinions keep you from reporting your abuse. I know this may not fit in this section of the book, but I also want to say to the abusers of same sex relationships, don't let those people's opinions keep you from coming out and asking for help and stopping the cycle of abuse.

- Maybe you feel that you are being punished for your sexual orientation.
- Maybe because you were assaulted by a same sex partner, you feel self loathing where it relates to your sexual orientation.
- Are you afraid if you admit to being abused by your same sex partner, you will be judged for being gay?

It doesn't matter if you are in a same sex relationship, you are entitled to the same rights as a victim as anyone else. There are people who believe that if you are in a same sex relationship, domestic violence can not exist. The truth is that there are almost as many domestic violence incidents in same sex relationship, than any other.

Never let shame of being in a same sex relationship keep you from reporting your abuse. A lot of people fear reporting their abuse because they are not sure how the authorities will react or they are afraid of their family's reaction. Maybe you have not come out to your family about your relationship. Please, do not let that also be a reason that you do not speak out on your situation.

There are a lot of reasons why people do not report their abuse. Trust that you are not alone. There are many resources that will help you get out of the dangerous situation you are in. If you are currently in an abusive relationship, you need to start making a safe exit plan. You must be careful. Your first step is talking to someone that you trust about your situation. If that person doesn't believe you or refuses to help you, go to someone else. Your safety is number one. It is very dangerous to be in an abusive relationship. It never gets better. It will only escalate and get worse.

Teen Abuse

Adults are not the only victims of abusive relationships. Female teens are also not the only people that are victims of abuse in teen relationships. These are all myths. Most of the time, teens are in the direct line of fire when it comes to abuse. When it comes to teen abuse, you have the issues of teens coming into maturity, so hormones are a factor, but should never be considered the reason. There is no acceptable excuse for abuse of any kind, in any relationship.

Most of the time, teens will hide the truth about their circumstances and the abuse because they are afraid of what others will think, or they are afraid of being alone. Maybe they grew up in an abusive household and to them, this may be the normal way to live their life. This is not the truth and should never be considered ok.

The following was taken from the website of the National Domestic Violence Hotline's website (NDVH).:

Dating Violence is a pattern of controlling behaviors that one partner uses to get power over the other and it includes:

- Any kind of physical violence or threat of physical violence to get control
- Emotional or mental abuse, such as playing mind games, making you feel crazy, constantly putting you down or criticizing you.
- Sexual abuse, including making you do anything you don't want to do, refusing to have safe sex or making you feel badly about yourself sexually.

Does your boyfriend/girlfriend:

- Have a history of bad relationships or past violence; always blaming his/her problems on other people, or blames you for "making" him/her treat you badly?
- Try to use drugs or alcohol to coerce you or get you alone when you don't want to be?
- Try to control you by being bossy, not taking your opinions seriously or making all of the

decisions about who or what you see, what you wear, what you do, etc?
- Talk negatively about people in a sexual way, or talk about sex like it's a game or contest?

Do you:

- Feel less confident about yourself when you are with him/her?
- Feel scared or worried about doing or saying "the wrong thing"?
- Find yourself changing behavior out of fear or to avoid a fight?

(NDVH)

These are all examples of situations that indicate you are in an abusive relationship. Don't be confused about your relationship because he/she has good days. This is very common, where a relationship has a lot of "good" days so a teen may try to disregard the "bad" days.

Please don't think you can change them. The time is not to change the situation. The abuse never gets better, but it certainly will get worse. You may think, oh he/she wouldn't act this way if he didn't care, or he/she is only protecting me. This is not the case at all. This is him/her being controlling and abusive. This is not love at all. This does not just end during the teen years. They do not "grow out" of this behavior. This will continue into adulthood if the abuser does not receive professional help and the victim doesn't realize it is happening and deciding to make a change.

Never assume that teen abuse only happens in heterosexual relationships. Gay, lesbian, bisexual, and transgender relationships also have to deal with these issues of abuse. No one is exempt from an abusive relationship.

Do you think you are alone? You are NOT!

- Nearly three in four tweens (72%) say boyfriend/girlfriend relationships usually begin at age 14 or younger. (Liz Claibourne Inc, study on teen dating abuse conducted by Teenage Research Unlimited, Feb 2008)
- 62% of tweens (age 11-14) who have been in a relationship say they know friends who have been verbally abused (called stupid, worthless, ugly, etc) by a boyfriend/girlfriend. (Liz Claibourne Inc, study on teen dating abuse conducted by Teenage Research Unlimited, Feb 2008)

- Only half of all tweens (age 11-14) claim to know the warning signs of a bad/hurtful relationship. (Liz Claibourne Inc, study on teen dating abuse conducted by Teenage Research Unlimited, Feb 2008)
- More than three times as many tweens (20%) as parents (6%) admit that parents know little or nothing about the tweens' dating relationships (Liz Claibourne Inc, study on teen dating abuse conducted by Teenage Research Unlimited, Feb 2008)
- 1 in 3 teenagers report knowing a friend or peer who has been hit, punched, kicked, slapped, choked, or physically hurt by their partner. (Liz Claibourne Inc, study on teen dating abuse conducted by Teenage Research Unlimited, Feb 2005)
- Nearly 1 in 5 teenage girls who have been in a relationship said a boyfriend had threatened violence or self-harm if presented with a break-up.(Liz Claibourne Inc, study on teen dating abuse conducted by Teenage Research Unlimited, Feb 2005)
- 13% of teenage girls who said they have been in a relationship reported being physically hurt or abused. (Liz Claibourne Inc, study on teen dating abuse conducted by Teenage Research Unlimited, Feb 2005)
- 1 in 4 teenage girls who have been in a relationship reveal that they have been pressured to perform oral sex or engage in intercourse. (Liz Claibourne Inc, study on teen dating abuse conducted by Teenage Research Unlimited, Feb 2005)

- More than 1 in 4 teenage girls in a relationship (26%) report enduring repeated verbal abuse. (Liz Claibourne Inc, study on teen dating abuse conducted by Teenage Research Unlimited, Feb 2005)
- 80% of teens regard verbal abuse as a "serious issue" for their age group. (Liz Claibourne Inc, study on teen dating abuse conducted by Teenage Research Unlimited, Feb 2005)
- If trapped in an abusive relationship, 73% of teens said they would turn to a friend for help; but only 33% who have been in or known about an abusive relationship said they have told anyone about it. (Liz Claibourne Inc, study on teen dating abuse conducted by Teenage Research Unlimited, Feb 2005)
- Twenty-four percent of 14 to 17-year-olds know at least one student who has been the victim of dating violence, yet 81% of parents either believe teen dating violence is not an issue or admit they don't know if it is an issue. (Survey commissioned by the Empower Program , sponsored by Liz Claibourne Inc, and conducted by Knowledge Networks, Social Control, Verbal Abuse, and Violence Among Teenager Research Unlimited, February 2005)
- Less than 25% of teens say they have discussed dating violence with their parents. (Liz Claibourne Inc, study of teens 13-17 conducted by Applied Research and Consulting LLC, Spring 2000)
- 89% of teens between the ages of 13 and 18 say thet have been in a dating relationship;

- 40% of teenage girls age 14-17 report knowing someone their age who has been hit or beaten by a boyfriend. (Children Now / Kaiser Permanente poll, December 1995)
- Nearly 80% of girls who have been physically abused in their intimate relationships continue to date their abuser. (City of New York, Teen Relationship Abuse Fact Sheet, March 1998)
- Of the women between the ages 15-19 murdered each year, 30% are killed by their husband or boyfriend. (City of New York, Teen Relationship Abuse Fact Sheet. March 1998

(www.DoSomething.org)

The National Domestic Violence Hotline has partnered with Liz Claibourne to create www.loveisrespect.org, The National Teen Dating Abuse Helpline (NTDAH). This is the only 24 hour helpline in the United States, that is dedicated to serving all 50 states, Puerto Rico, and the Virgin Islands.

Chapter 3

The After School Gang

In the following chapters, you will read about my personal experiences of abuse as a child. I write my experiences for you, the readers. I pray that listening to some of my stories, I can help you or someone you know in dealing with their feelings and their traumas

I attended, Hart School, in Stamford, CT. This was my first and last year attending Hart School. This was also my first year attending school, I was in kindergarten and 5 years old. Although, I lived across town from the school, I still didn't take the bus. Either a parent or one of my sisters had to walk me to school and pick me up. This would be the beginning of many incidences of negative bouts of abuse.

There were a group of guys, about 3-4, that knew one of my sisters. To this day, I only know one of them due to a conversation that I had with a few people. Depending on who picked me up from school, that would decide on how my afternoon would be. If only something were said sooner, maybe it could have saved a lot of time and emotions from being felt.

I was guaranteed to see this group of males anytime school was in session as they have issues of some sort with one of my sisters. They would wait for us to be down the street from my school before approaching us. I would often beg my sister to walk the other way to go home and she would always say, no we are going to walk this way.

Located down the street and around the corner, was an old office building. This would be the place we would meet when they wanted to "talk". They always separated us. We were always separated once we arrived. We were never allowed to remain together. I could not hear or see her. I didn't want to be separated from her. I did not know these guys and personally, I didn't want to. I never knew their names. All I wanted, was to go home.

They would start by leaving me with one guy, while the rest of them went elsewhere. I started getting a very uneasy feeling. He would start asking me questions that eventually lead to him standing over me as I stood with my back against the wall. He would place his hand on the wall above me and just hover there as he spoke to me. He would hold my arm with his other hand. He would start telling me how pretty I was as he would let go of my arm and start running his hand down my face and continue down my arms and then my body, to places he should never be touching. I wanted my sister. Once again, I just wanted to go home.

Everyday, after school, I would ask my sister to walk a different and faster way home, I never understood why she always told me, we had to go the other way. I hated it! She never said ok. Years later, according to her, she was a victim of theirs as well.

Then the day came where we got the courage to tell someone, our mom and my dad. They called a police detective (I believe he was a detective at the time) and we told him about what was going on. He said that he would speak to them and take care of it. The next day my sister and I were called to our living room. We were told by the same detective that he himself spoke to them and due to lack of evidence, there was nothing he could do. It was our word against theirs.

Was he kidding? He did not seem like it. If you can't tell the police, who can you tell? So, now are we the liars in the situation? I know what I've gone through. I know what has happened to me. I know what I've been told. I now know that no matter what I say, there is nothing that can be done. Who am I going to run to for help? Who is going to be that way out? Here I am, a five year old child who is going through something children are told to report because you will always be believed and yet here we are and there is nothing to be done.

There were repercussions for talking to the police. We were always separated. The fondling got more intense. The tone in their voices got deeper and angrier sounding. I, myself was even cuter now. Cute enough that each day, there was a different person "staying" with me and expressing how cute I was.

I was thankful for the weekends. I got a break from them. I was even more grateful and happy when I changed schools at the end of the school year. They would come to our block, but they weren't welcome by everyone for different reasons. Home was my safe haven, or so I thought. As stated before, in the next few chapters, you will see that home wasn't a safe haven after all.

CHAPTER 4

The Monster In The Hallway

Carlos was a neighbor that lived behind us. There were a row of trees that divided our backyard from the house behind us. My grandmother also lived in one of the apartments on the first floor of the house. He lived on the second floor. No one knew what would happen in the halls. No one knew about the monster in the hallway.

My mother never liked him. I'm not even sure that she knew a true reason why. She would say that she didn't like how he acted. I just know she never had any use for him. There was nothing anyone could do to change her mind either. Little did she know, she had a very good reason for disliking him.

I remember having a good friend that lived in that house as well. She moved away and to this day, I pray she never had to encounter him in a negative way. I pray that no other child had to either. If I had to sacrifice myself so that no other child was in harms way, that's what I was willing to do.

Many times, I just wanted that house to vanish. I wanted all of my loved ones to move out and move somewhere so they never had to be in his presence. I didn't even want him to be able to look at them. I didn't want them to possibly have to endure his evil ways.

I can not tell you when the hall encounters with Carlos began. I remember being very young. I can wish it never happened, but I can not change the past. It is what it is. I can only learn and move on. I can tell you when it ended though, but that will be later in this chapter.

The hallways were dark, if only there were light. Would that help? Would that prevent the monster from lurking in the night? Maybe people would have seen something or would have been there. Light in the hallways wouldn't have made people walk the halls. If people were going to use those halls at those times, they would have used them anyways. I learned that early on when it came to my interactions with Carlos. It wouldn't matter what, he made it clear that he will have a "meeting" with me when he feels the time is appropriate. I didn't know when the next time would be until I saw him. He would make it known when the time was right.

I remember him opening the door to his apartment, just as I would walk by. The first time this occurred, nothing happened. He would just open the door, see who was walking by and then close the door. I just thought he was being nosey. These events would lead to the beginning of many more events to occur.

I can remember walking through the door leading into the hallway, going to visit a friend and finding Carlos sitting on the stairway. He was just sitting there, like he was bored with nothing to do. Looking back, I sometimes think and I wonder if he was waiting for me, so he would have something to do.

There was a specific day, when my mom, sisters and I were laying out in the backyard. There is a concrete wall that stretched down across from the trees that separated the two properties and run along the driveway to the connecting street. Carlos would come outside and sit on the wall watching us. He wouldn't even try to hide the fact that he was watching us. For me, this was my cue that it was time for a meeting. To my mother, it meant chasing the creepy neighbor guy away with a machete for looking at her children.

I knew that by the next day, I had to visit my friend. After a while, my friend's family moved. I had to just make up excuses on why I disappeared. My main excuse was,"Oh I was at the park." or "I was walking around." I was able to use those excuses due to how the neighborhood was built. The time would come for me to attend my meeting.

I would walk through the door into the hallway and he would make a noise in the darkness to let me know he was there. I would walk towards him and just want to cry. He would make me feel so uncomfortable, and that was even before he started the unimaginable events. What's a very young girl to do? As you have already read, the police can't do anything. It would be his word versus mine, and I already heard the outcome of that. What's the point?

He would start by either making me sit next to him on the stairs, or stand in front of him, with my back to him. If I were sitting next to him, he would start by rubbing my leg and running his hand along my inner thighs, while telling me open my legs. He would continue to touch me over my clothes while telling me it was our secret because no one would understand. Wow, where have I heard that before?

He wasn't done there. He wanted more! He wanted me to stand in front of him on the stairs while facing him. Carlos showed me how he liked his manhood to be rubbed over his clothes. If that isn't enough, I had to turn around and face away from him while standing on the stairs. I remember thinking, "oh please don't let me fall down these stairs." Something inside always told me that I would never have that problem because he always had a hold of me. Once I turned around, he would put his arm around me. He always placed his hands around my waist. He would continue to hold me as he used his other hand to explore the inside of my panties until he reached the place, no one should ever touch a child or any other adult that doesn't want to be touched. He would continue to rub me until he decided it was time to stop. I would ask him to stop and he would inform me that he will stop when he is ready to and until then, I will do as he tells me too. Who was I to try and stop him? It wasn't like I had the ability to stop him anyways. It wasn't like anyone was going to be able to stop him.

He would tell me how much of a good girl I was. I could never tell anyone because then, I would be a bad girl and no one would believe me. He would also let me know that no one believes children anyways. Oh how I know this to be true. Another reason I couldn't tell anyone was because he knew where I was and if I were a bad girl, I would be dealt with like a bad girl is dealt with. He never told me details about what exactly that entailed but I didn't want to know either.

According to him, it was normal for boys and girls, to do this kind of thing. This is something I later heard from others that wanted to indulge in this type of foreplay. After a while, you really do begin to believe the things you hear.

I remember one time, a family member of mine, came into the hall while I was in a meeting. I was facing away from Carlos and I told the family member to go around to the other side of the house and use the stairs. They kept asking me what I was doing and I said I was playing. I was playing on these stairs and they had to go around because I didn't want them on my stairs. Carlos had his hands down my pants and I could feel his grip getting tighter. The family member got irritated, but eventually did leave. Looking back now, that could have been a moment to say something, but I couldn't. Carlos knew where I was at all times.

The time came that ended Carlos' abuse. I didn't want to see him, I knew it was time to save myself because no one else was going to. I wasn't going to show up. It would be taking a big chance if this didn't work. Good thing for me it did. At least where Carlos was concerned.

I was eating an apple and I lost my two front teeth. I went and told someone (honestly, don't remember who), that Carlos just hit me and now my teeth were missing. The next thing I know, my mother is running down the street, and the police were there. I told the police that Carlos had hit me.

Some would ask me, why I didn't just tell them about the sexual abuse, and honestly, I wish I did. At the time, I was given every reason to not say anything. This was working for me at the time. I know I can't have everything my way, so maybe this was one of those times. I now know this to not be true.

The last thing I remember hearing about Carlos is that he was being sent to the hospital for evaluation. When people from the neighborhood heard what I did and how I had him arrested for physical assault, I was called a liar, mean person, and someone who just ruined an innocent man's life. If they only knew what kind of man the "Monster In The Hallway" really was.

You're allowed
to scream,
You're allowed
to cry,
but do not give up

~ Author Unknown

CHAPTER 5

Two Pathways To Abuse

Like I said earlier in this book, the street I lived on was a dead end street and everyone knew everyone and Mark was no exception. He lived two houses over from me. From what I hear now, I wasn't the first girl he tried anything with. I'm not sure if he was successful with anyone else. I do hope that no one has had to experience his advances or anything of the sort.

Mark lived in a house where it was more of a rooming house. You had a single room but you shared the kitchen and bath with other people. I had known plenty of other people in that house, but Mark was different then the rest.

He would always have people come over. There were always people out on my street and it was no big deal if all of the kids went into everyone's house. Everyone would watch over everyone. No one knew there were those that wanted to watch others a little to close.

Mark had his own separate entrance besides the main door to go into the house. There were plenty of times that I totally avoided going near that door. It didn't matter. There were always other doors. To the right of the main door, set back a little was his private entrance. Once you go into the main door, his room was the first door to the right. There was back doors down the hallways, but they weren't always the safest way to go.

There were numerous times, Mark wanted me to come to his room. After a while, it became normal, just like every other time. Mark would have me come to his for the most part to "hang out", but that was in the beginning. Then after a while, he wasn't the cool guy anymore. He wasn't safe anymore. He wasn't the friendly, kid safe neighbor that everyone imagined him to be.

The first time I realized, Mark wasn't like everyone else, I was caught off guard. He was the cool guy. He was the one that was always out in public, on the street having fun, and full of laughs wanting to have a good time. Little did anyone know, he was no better than anyone else. He was actually just another one of those people. He wasn't mean about anything, well not at first.

I was there, in his room hanging out with other people and other kids. Like I said, everyone used to just walk into other people's homes and think nothing of it. If the door was open, the home was open. As people started to leave, I was asked to stay and hang out. Looking back now, I can see all of the signs of what not to do. They were as clear as a bell. None of this was and still is not my fault. This was something I took a while to learn.

I stayed behind. I was only there by myself for a few minutes. I got up to leave and he stopped me. I thought he was joking, so I tried to pull away. He grabbed me tighter and took me back to the bed. He hovered over me before starting to kiss me and rub his hands over my body. He never placed his hands under my clothes, but this doesn't make it less offensive. When he was done, he told me to not tell anyone. It was our secret. Once again, no one would believe me. Once again I believed him. I mean, what else could I do? I attribute all of these years of keeping secrets as to why I am so good and listening to others and keeping their secrets.

He always found a way to get me to his room. One time a friend of mine and I were walking through the back door of the house to the front, to take a short cut. Just before we got to his door, he opened it and invited us in. I tried getting her to keep going, but she agreed to go in. Everyone knew him, or so they thought. I thought she would be my ticket to not going in. We went into his room as he told us it would be ok to sit on the bed and relax. I had gone through this before and I didn't want her to have to go through what I encountered almost every day. I almost told her to just go ahead without me, but then again, she may have started asking questions and I just didn't want to tell anyone. Obviously, there was nothing that can be done about it.

Her mom had called her home. She got up to go home and then asked if I was going to go with her. I thought about it, but looking to Mark, I can see the answer was no. I let her know that since she had to go home for the day/night, I would just stay for a little while longer. What else could I do? I could have made a scene about going, but then maybe get questioned about it later, only to be told, it doesn't matter because there was nothing that could be done. I would rather just deal with it. This was nothing new to me.

There were numerous times, Mark wanted me to come to his room. After a while, it became normal, just like every other time. Mark would have me come to his for the most part to "hang out", but that was in the beginning. Then after a while, he wasn't the cool guy anymore. He wasn't safe anymore. He wasn't the friendly, kid safe neighbor that everyone imagined him to be.

To this day, I don't know why Mark stopped abusing me. He just did. No rime or reason, that I know of. This went on for a while, so the reason for him stopping, are still, to this day a mystery for me. He just stopped talking to me altogether. Please don't misunderstand me, it didn't bother me that he did stop, but it's not very common, in my experience and from those that I have spoken to, that pedophiles, rapists, abusers, and the like, just stop like that.

I pray that Mark was able to find peace and happiness within himself and I pray that no other person had to endure any mental or physical abuse at the hands of Mark. If they did, I pray that they realize their self worth and are able to rise above all of the hurt and pain. May they realize that out of every tragic past, there is a positive future.

Just because you can't see the positive

side of every negative action, doesn't

mean there isn't one.

~Stacy Lupinacci

CHAPTER 6

The Unknown Sibling

    This may in fact be the shortest story that I have, but it is a story in my life. The unknown sibling is called such because because no one can remember him. He even had the same last name as she did. They called themselves brother and sister. It seems like no one knows of his existence, everyone, except me.

    His name is Jackson. When I first met him, he seemed like a cool guy. He was actually one of two siblings of a neighbor. At least that's what they considered themselves. That's what they were introduced to us as, siblings. I was informed by his sister that he was a good guy and she loved the fact that he was there visiting. With that being said, Jackson was more then curious about getting to know me, right from the beginning.

    I remember Jackson sitting on the stairs right outside of our apartment door that went upstairs. We live on the bottom floor, in the only apartment in the house. There were rooms for rent upstairs that had to share a bathroom. Then there was the "attic" which had to more private rooms for someone to live in. The way our room was, if you sat on the stairs outside of our front door, you could see directly to where my bed was.

It wasn't too long after meeting Jackson, that I saw him sitting on the stairs. He was holding a deck of playing cards. He would show me the ace of hearts and give me the sign that meant, I love you. He would point to his eye, then to either his heart or the heart on the card, and then to me. I thought this was weird but it was funny. This was different for me, so I didn't see it as a sign of what was to come later.

I started laughing at him. Seriously, I was about seven or eight years old, and how can he love me. Some would say to me, "Stacy, how do you know what love is at that age? The fact is that even at such a young age, I had been subjected to adult situations, that most people in their twenties have experienced. So young, yet so knowledgeable. I knew things at that age that children shouldn't even know about. Those were different times.

In the coming days, I would come to find out just how much he loved me. The first time I had a physical encounter, which wasn't just a friendly manner, was a few days after meeting Jackson. His sister had asked him to go to her room and get something for her. I had been up there earlier and knew what she was talking about and where it was, so I said that I would get it. Jackson said that he would go with me and let me in. Once inside her room, I got the item she needed and tried to leave. He was in the doorway and started telling me how pretty I was. I laughed and said, "I know". He moved only a few inches to let me by, but it was enough for me to get through, although I had to brush up against him to get through. I didn't think anything of it and we went back downstairs.

The next incident was when I went upstairs, looking for his sister. I knocked on her door, and he answered and said she wasn't home. I ended up sticking around and talking to Jackson. I was sitting on a mattress on the floor when he came and started a pillow fight with me. At one point, I went to hit him with the pillow and I lost my balance. I stumbled into him and he caught me, but that wasn't the end of it. He leaned over and kissed me on the lips. I froze and couldn't grasp what just happened. He looked at me and told me that he wouldn't do anything I didn't want him to do. This was the first time anyone ever told me that. I was used to the same statements, "Do it because everyone else is doing it.", Do it because I said so.", or "Do it or else". Not once did Jackson ever tell me that he would hurt me, or threaten me if I didn't do it. He was always friendly and always had a pleasant tone in his voice. I have heard over the years of my abuse life, that this was the normal thing everyone was doing. Then I see these acts of affection in public and everyone really IS enjoying themselves, so maybe THIS is what everyone is really doing. It didn't seem like I should be doing it, but who knows? I know that I didn't like every other person's story about what everyone was doing. I also knew that I didn't like everyone being mean and would say negative things to me and about my family. I continued to kiss him. He would ask me how I learned to kiss like that. I just didn't want to answer him. I kept kissing him and he would hold me tighter, but it wasn't like anything else I had experienced.

    Jackson was too nice to mean anything in a negative way. Maybe what he was saying was the truth. Maybe everyone was doing this, but the others were just to mean about it. My gut instinct was that maybe something was wrong and this wasn't right either, but this was something a little different, so maybe it wasn't wrong after all. It was nice to not be threatened and his sister did say that he was a good guy. She would know better than me. Maybe this is what people were doing and not the mean and vulgar way of interacting with others.

    Jackson would be in the hallways or on the porch, talking with other people from the neighborhood. I would glance at him and get the "nod" to come sit by him. My choices were clear. I could either sit by Jackson or have to go and deal with other people. I didn't want that. If I had to deal with the other people that were always negative and mean to me, I choose Jackson.

When Jackson first came to visit his sister, he came with another brother, whose name I can't remember. One day, we all went to the movies. Jackson sat between his brother and myself. The other brother never even noticed that Jackson would hold my hand. Our hands were placed on the seats in between us.

Although what we were doing was wrong, I couldn't resist the fact that Jackson always made it about me. It was always about my happiness. Was it wrong? Sure it was, but that the time, I was "happy" that he was different and he wasn't mean. It doesn't mean it was right, but it does lesson the emotional and physical fear. It also gives me a break from the rest of the evil society. If I had to choose between the two evils, I pick this one. This ended due to Jackson going back home. As much as it was wrong, I missed him. Especially when I had to deal with the others. He was different than the other monsters I had to encounter. He wasn't mean. He didn't threaten me. He didn't make me fear him like the others. There was a nurturing quality to him that I would never find in any of the others.

There is always light at the end of the

tunnel. You just have to feel your way

through the tunnel to get to the

golden pot at the end of the rainbow,

Which sometimes falls over the tunnel,

Making it hard to see.

~ Stacy Lupinacci

CHAPTER 7

Who Was He?

When it comes to Juan, I really don't know what to say. Well I know what to say, just not sure how to say it. Depending on you talk to, depends on who he was. I don't remember his last name. I knew it at one time, but can't remember it now. Come to think about it, no one can.

The story of who Juan was or where he came from is a mystery to everyone. It is also a good thing that people do remember that he actually existed. If not, I may start to think he was a figment of my imagination. I know he was real, but after Jackson and no one remembering him, I don't know if I can deal with another one that no one remembers.

I still can't figure out which sister he was dating. I thought it may have been both, but I have been informed it was only one. There is still a discrepancy on which one it was. They both say the other but never both. The real question is, "Who was he really?"

He didn't live in our neighborhood, but he did show up almost day. There were days that I didn't have to have any interactions with him, but it wasn't enough. Those days were far and few between. Days like these are when I wished Jackson were here. Especially when things with Juan got worse.

I remember the first time I had an encounter with Juan, one that was inappropriate. He never took the time to warm up to the idea of not even getting caught. I can not tell you the scenario either. All I remember is being in the living room with family members and Juan. One of my family members even witnessed the following events. Some years ago, they brought to my attention that they remembered what happened. To ask them now, I don't know. I believe they do.

Every time we were left alone, he felt it necessary to express how cute I was. Here we go again! He would ask me if I had any little boyfriends from the neighborhood. He would constantly give me compliments. This was not Jackson. It just wasn't the same. Although he didn't mention anything negative, I got the worse vibes from him. Nothing from him expressed the friendliest of people either.

At one point he came to me when we were alone, and told me to hurry up and give him my hand. He had a surprise for me. Can I get a break? When I wouldn't give him my hand, he took it and rubbed my hand across his pants over his groin area. He would get close to my ear and moan, telling me how good I make him feel. If only someone would just walk in, this would all end. This could be my way out. I wouldn't have to tell anyone. It would all come out on it's own. The moment never came and in fact, years later, it almost happens again. I'll write more about that later.

    He was brave. He was bold. He was demanding. Juan would tell me that my age would keep anyone from believing me. Now, this I DID believe. After my previous encounters, I knew what Juan was saying was the truth. No one would believe me. Now I know different. There are people out there who will believe you no matter what your age is. Find and trust that person.

    Every interaction with him was a little more intense until the unthinkable happened. He came over and I was in the living room with a family member. Juan told me to get in front of him and grab a blanket. What is he planning now and why? We weren't alone. He had me grab a crocheted blanket and throw it on the family member who was younger than me. I had another blanket to cover us. He stood behind me and whispered in my ear to hold the blanket because he was going to pull my pants down. I didn't know what to say. Then he would grab me by my hips and pull me closer. He told me to lean over and make sure the other person in the room didn't take the blanket off. I didn't want this. I didn't know what he was doing, and personally, I didn't like it.

I could feel his penis against my body and him pulling my hips closer to him. I tried to move and squiggle, trying to make him let me go but he grabbed me closer. Then I tried to stand up and he whispered in my ear that if I didn't lean back over and do my job, I was going to get hurt. What was he trying to do. Then, I started crying as an unbelievable and overbearing pain hit me, he penetrated my vagina. I started to cry but had to keep it quiet and he told me to laugh, so I did. He didn't want anyone to think I was upset and that he hurt me. When he was done, he pulled my pants back up and said he had to go. I didn't see him again after that day, not until years later.

I was 15 years old and in tenth grade. I was walking through the halls when I really should have been in class. To this day, I can't remember why I wasn't in class. I just remember walking the hall. I was walking near the stairs that lead up to the theater area. Someone walks up to me, and grabs my arm telling me to go with him. I looked to see who it was and it was Juan.

How did he know where I was or who I was. I still don't know the answer to that question. The truth is that he did know who I was and he was clear that he wanted me to go with him. We went up to the theater room. I didn't want to go. I started shaking and wanted to cry. My last encounter with this person was the worst experience ever.

We got into the theater room and there was a couch in there. He threw me on the couch, got on top of me and started to kiss me but I started crying. I couldn't kiss him the way he wanted me to. He told me to take off my pants. I said no that I didn't want to be hurt again. He held me by my throat and told me to do what he said. I started to take my pants down and he slipped his hand from my throat down my pants. Within minutes, my prayers had been answered because we thought we heard someone coming to the room we were in. Just jumped off of me and disappeared. I never saw him again, not even to this day.

Like a flower in the desert

I had to grow

in the cruelest weather

holding on to every drop of rain

just to stay alive

But it's not enough to survive,

I want to bloom

beneath the blasting sun,

and show you all of the colors

that live inside of me,

I want you to see

what I can become.

~ Christy Ann Martine

CHAPTER 8

It Isn't All Sexual Abuse

I had been keeping to myself and I did not want to get into a relationship. I was focused on work. I was fed up with trying to make relationships work. I was tired of trying to figure out what was wrong with me and why I was having such a bad time with relationships. I understand that everyone is not perfect and I am pretty sure I am included in that, but I did not see what I was doing wrong. It was time for me to not bother getting into another relationship.

I met TJ through a friend named Scott. Scott thought it would be a good idea for him to set me up on a blind date. I despised blind dates, but I would make an exception this one time. This friend had insisted that he had the perfect guy for me and although I have never been into the "perfect" guy, I finally gave in and agreed to meet, TJ for dinner.

Scott had told me that TJ had just broke up with his girlfriend because he found she had been cheating on him. I had informed Scott that I did not think it was a good idea since he just got out of a relationship. Scott insured me that TJ was ready for a new relationship. He had been done with his ex for a few weeks. Ok I will give it a try. I told Scott to give TJ my number and we will see how it goes.

TJ called me three days later and we agreed to meet and have dinner. I got to the restaurant early and waited where I could see the front entrance. I saw who I wanted to be TJ enter the restaurant about 10 minutes before our agreed time. Could it be him? He was alone. I waited about 8 mins or so before going in.

I walked in and told the hostess that I was meeting someone. She asked me what the name was of the person was meeting. I informed her and she walked me to our table. It was him, the guy I saw walk in ten minutes ago. He was even more beautiful face to face. I thought he was the most beautiful guy I've seen. TJ, stood about 6'2". He had dark brown hair and green eyes. To say that I was impressed, was an understatement. This is all fine and good, but would he be all looks and not what I wanted anyways.

Scott must have told TJ that I liked flowers and what kind because TJ handed me a single Fire and Ice rose wrapped in baby's breath. He said that he hoped I like it. He wasn't sure if he should get me a Stargazer Lilly, a Sunflower, or a Fire and Ice rose. Yeah, he just happened to know my favorite flowers (oh sure....I will get with Scott later on how he knew them. Later, Scott did in fact admit to telling him, but it was only after TJ asked him).

He was such a gentleman. We had a lovely dinner and got to know each other a little before leaving the restaurant. We decided to walk along the beach. We walked, talked and played in the sand for a few hours before calling it a night. As we were walking back to the parking lot, we talked about how much fun we had and agreed to meet up again.

I couldn't wait to get home and call Scott and thank him for his efforts Scott was laughing as he answered the phone. The funny thing was, TJ had already called him thanking him for setting us up to meet. TJ was a long time friend of Scott. Scott told me that he didn't like TJ's ex girlfriend and he was happy that we got along. The one thing I didn't know until about two dates with TJ later, was that Scott told TJ the same thing about my ex-boyfriend. He didn't like him either.

TJ and I went out a few times before he asked me to be his girlfriend. I really enjoyed being with him and the times we spent together, so why not? Things were great. A few months went by and I couldn't believe how great things were going. Could I have found a genuine gem in a pile of painted rocks?

About seven months went by and things were great. We have had a few disagreements, but they were nothing and we moved on from them and continued to live our lives and be happy. Nothing that any couple doesn't go through, right? We loved each other and nothing was going to change that. I was actually beginning to think that TJ could be "the one". TJ had been telling me how much he loves everything about me, even the little things I did that irritated him. He said my little imperfections are what made me unique as well as all of the love I had to give. He accepted me as I was. He didn't care that I wasn't a size 6. He didn't care that I wasn't perfect according to everyone else's standards. I was perfect for him. He always told me how much I meant to him and I appreciated hearing it. I couldn't help but tell him how much he meant to me as well.

We would compliment each other on what we were wearing and everything. There were times, if he didn't like what I was wearing, I would change. If he didn't like certain friends or they didn't like him, I would have to keep them separated and could not hang out with them at the same time. This became very tiresome for me. Trying to please everyone at the same time. When did this start because I've never cared to before. Maybe it was because I was in love with him and I knew that there were things that I had to do to make a relationship work. A relationship is about give and take, isn't it? How much giving do you do before you realize that you give more than you take? When do you realize that what you do take is not what you should be taking?

TJ and I had been taking turns staying at each others apartment. We spent all of our time together. Of course we spent time with our friends apart, and went to work, but we were together a lot. One day, TJ came over after a bad day at work. I had talked to him earlier that day and we agreed that we would go out for dinner. We were talking about where we wanted to go. He seemed a little agitated from the moment he walked in. I wanted to make his evening better than his day.

He became argumentative over a question I asked him and decided he was going to leave. I asked him to explain what was really wrong and to not leave. He left anyways. I didn't hear from him for a few hours. I started to get worried because this was so out of character for him. I haven't seen him this upset and angry. I even tried to call Scott and get his advice. Scott said he would try to contact him and see what's going on.

Scott called me back and said that he talked to TJ and he actually seemed fine. He didn't seem angry or anything. I asked Scott if he was sure he was talking to the same TJ that was just here. He laughed and said yes. I was confused. I didn't know what else to say.

A few hours later, TJ called me saying he was coming back over and I was happy to hear from him. I was still confused, but happy to hear from him. TJ got back to my apartment and laid on my bed, saying he was tired. I wanted to talk about what had happened earlier and where he had been. I also wanted to know why Scott thought he was just fine and I know he left in a not so good mood.

I told TJ to talk to me and I wasn't letting him go to sleep until he did so. He looked at me with a different look in his eyes. He wasn't the loving guy I knew. This was more then him just putting his foot down and disagreeing with me. His whole persona seemed to change in just a few hours. There was something different about him.

I do not know what came over me, but something told me to ask him one question. I decided to go ahead and ask him, "Who is she?" I can not begin to tell you the energy shift that took place at that moment. He jumped up, looked at me and told me to never accuse him of anything like that ever again. He walked out of the room, but those that know me, know that is NOT the end of that conversation. I followed behind him demanding that he tell me what was going on and asking if there were someone. He kept telling me to back off. I had infidelity issues with past relationships and I refused to deal with that again.

TJ tried to grab his jacket to leave and I took the jacket from him and told him that he needed to talk to me and be honest. He was not very happy with me as he turned around, looked me right in the eyes and told me to back off and never talk to him like that again. I couldn't even begin to say what exactly was going through my mind at that time. I can say what I think I was thinking. I can tell you that I did not care to stop and think that I'm only 5'4" and here he is over 6ft tall, construction worker built and not in the best of moods. He turned around to open the door and I got in front of him and slammed the door shut, demanding that he man up and talk to me. He dropped what he had in his hands, picked me up by my arms and threw me up against the wall. I shoved him back and told him to never put his hands on me again. He slapped me and took me to the bedroom and threw me on the bed. He told me that he will do who and what he wants and I will not question him on anything, ever again. He walked out the door.

What could or should I do? What did I just hear? I was crushed. I felt like my heart was just ripped out and handed to me in the worse way. I gave everything I had to him. He was all that I wanted in a man and I didn't understand what was going on. I laid on my bed and I cried for what seemed like hours. I didn't know what to do. I wanted to call him but as I cried because I was hurt, I was also so mad that I allowed it to go that far. I was mad at myself and I was mad at him. What should I be feeling? I was angry but more than anything, I was hurt. Once I stopped hurting, all I could do was sit there in the quiet, still of darkness and think. I had to think of what to do. I couldn't talk to anyone. I couldn't even call Scott. If Scott knew that TJ had caused me physical harm, that would have caused a major altercation between the two of them. Scott was so anti domestic violence on women and I didn't want them to fight.

What did I do to make him so angry? What did I do to make him want to step out of our relationship? What did I do to make him cross the line and become physically abusive? Maybe I should have just let him go.

As I sat there and thought about what I could have done differently, I decided that I would give TJ some space. This was not the TJ, I knew. This was not the TJ, I was in love with. There must be something we can do to work this out.

A few days passed and TJ called me. I cried when I heard his voice. The guy I was talking to, was the guy I was in love with. He said he wanted to come to my place and explain what happened. I missed him. I wanted to hold him. I wanted to work everything out. Was this even possible? I didn't know, but I was willing to try.

TJ arrived moments later. He walked in and wrapped his arms around me and told me how sorry he was. He told me that he had made a huge mistake and wanted to talk about it. He confessed that he went out that night to hang with his friends and got introduced to another woman and after a few drinks, he had sex with her. He also continued to claim that he got so angry, not at me, but he was angry with himself for doing what he did and when he saw me and how I reacted to him, he felt horrible and instead of being so mad at himself, he took it out on me. He saw my anger at him as a way of him yelling at himself and he was already trying to deal with the guilt.

I did not believe him, so I started asking him about the attitude he had when he first got to my apartment. He said, at that point, he just had a really bad day and didn't mean to take it out on me. I wasn't sure that I believed him, but I accepted his apology anyways.

Time went by and things with TJ were great. Every day was worked on getting over what happened. In the back of my mind, I worried about it happening again. I been through infidelity in relationships before and did not want to deal with it anymore. If he wasn't in the best of moods, I just let him have his space. I didn't want to make the mistake of something happening again and it be my fault.

I always swore that I would never be in an abusive relationship. I've seen it too many times in my life with different people and I swore I would never be like them and allow that kind of thing. I didn't see this as allowing it. I saw it as giving him and our relationship a second chance.

I remember one day I was going out with some friends. I asked TJ if I looked good. I didn't know if I was really liking my outfit, so I thought to ask TJ for his opinion. He didn't like it, so I changed. He didn't like the next two outfits I chose to wear, so I changed. After a few hours he started calling around trying to get ahold of me. These were the days of pagers. I checked my pager and in a matter of a couple hours, he had over 10 pages waiting for me return.

I decided to go home and when I walked in my apartment, he started yelling at me. He was asking me where I went and who I was with. I tried to tell him but he didn't look like he believed me. He said that if I ever cheated on him, he wouldn't give me the second chance like I gave him. I informed him that I didn't need a second chance because I wasn't doing anything wrong.

Time went on and TJ started to get more controlling. He started demanding to know where I was going, who I was going with and what I was wearing. At the time, I thought it was just his own insecurities coming back at him because of what he did. I came up with every excuse out there to justify why it was ok for him to treat me like that. I did not allow anyone else to tolerate this kind of treatment in their relationship, but I was blind to the severity of my own situation with TJ. I was in love with him and since I am always fighting to the end, there was a way to work through this.

The final straw came when TJ and I both decided one night that we were both going to go out with friends together for a while and then breaking off with our friends separately. We went out to dinner with friends and during dinner, everything was great. He decided to go hang out with the guys and I went with the ladies. We drove around for a while, went to one of their house for a few hours and then I went home.

I didn't hear from TJ since we separated earlier. I paged TJ when I got home and didn't hear back from him until he walked in the door. Once again, he seemed like he was irritated. I asked how his night with the guys went. He claimed that it was great but I wouldn't understand because I was too worried about wanting to be with a guy in the restaurant we were all at earlier. I asked him how many drinks did he have when he was out with the boys, because he wasn't making any sense.

TJ informed me that there was a guy that kept looking at me and I was always smiling at him every chance I got. I couldn't remember any guy at the restaurant, except for the waiter because honestly, I wasn't paying attention to anyone else. Later, TJ started yelling at me, accusing me of flirting with the waiter and wanting to be with him. I smiled at him too much. I tried to explain to him that it was polite to smile and acknowledge someone when they are talking to you. He informed me that I pushed him too far and he thought he could trust me. He thought I loved him. He thought I was different then his ex and he thought he could spend the rest of his life with me. Then the pager went off, and he had to call his "boy".

What the heck was going on? He actually had me thinking about earlier that night and how I had been acting. I was actually beginning to think I may have done something wrong. I could hear him talking on the phone saying they were going out the next night after work for a few drinks and at the point, I was more concerned about our conversation before he called his friend. Then TJ got quiet, but I could hear him talking but it was like a whisper. I walked up to the entrance to the room he was in and just listened. I heard those words that proved he wasn't talking to his, "boy". As I listened I heard, "So, what are you wearing?" I walked up to him and without a warning I said, "Why do you want to know what your boy is wearing?" and I grabbed MY phone. As I said hello, TJ pushed me out of the way and left. I had a wonderful conversation with a woman who informed me that she met TJ when he was out with his friends and she thought that he was single. I realized this was the same woman he had cheated on me with prior. I asked her about that night she met him and she told me everything. She swore on everything that she believed in that she thought he was single. I informed her that he in fact was very much taken, but only up until that conversation with her. I let her know that she was free to have him. I was done with him and his attitude, cheating ways, the accusations, and the obsessions with who I talk to and how I dress.

    The next day, I was in my kitchen, starting to cook dinner, when TJ walked in. We were loud. That was not a quiet conversation! He started yelling at me, accusing me of ruining his life and that I had no right to talk to his "friend". I told him we were over and he needed to leave. There was no more talking about it. He needed to get his belongings and leave. He grabbed me and threatened to beat the shit out of me for acting like a bitch. I pushed him back and warned him to get out. He came back and slapped me across my face, hard enough to throw me off my feet. I fell to the ground and he kicked me as he continued to yell at me how I ruined his life and I will always be by myself because I make people cheat on me. I make people do things to me and maybe if I wasn't a fat, insecure bitch, who didn't know how to mind my own business, I would know a good man when I see them and keep them. As he walked away, he made sure that I heard him tell me that I was probably never raped and that I actually wanted to be raped and molested. He should have known I was going to be a whore and sleep with everyone and anyone.

I started crying. I couldn't believe what was happening. What was he talking about? How could he say all of those mean things? He was taking everything I told him and using it against me. I got up from the floor to check on the pot of water. I had just turned the pot on when he walked in and everything seemed to happen so fast.

TJ walked into the kitchen and started yelling in my face again. I pushed him back with everything I had into the wall. As he came back at me, I grabbed the pot of water and threw it at him. Then I grabbed the frying pan and commenced to hitting him with it. I was crying. I was at my ropes end. I was done. He put his hand on my for me last time. He broke my heart for the last time. He went too far this time.

He tried to leave without his belongings. When he walked out of the door, I dropped the frying pan and just cried. I didn't know what was worse. Everything that he just said and did to me, or me hitting the man I was in love with. No matter how I felt about him, it had to end. I noticed his things sitting in the kitchen. I took them and threw them out the front door. I didn't want him to have any reason to come back.

I never saw him again. A few years later, the girl that worked for me, informed me that I had a phone call. The person on the phone wouldn't tell her who he was. I answered the phone and it was TJ. The first thing he said, was, "Stacy, please do not hang up on me. I really need to talk to you." I asked him how he found me and he stated that you can find almost anyone now a days if you really want to. I asked him what he wanted that he had to track me down and talk to me. He wanted to apologize for everything that happened between us. He said he ended up going into counseling for a few things and had to address this part of his life because I was a major positive influence to him and he ruined it.

TJ apologized for calling me all of the names he did, the last time we saw each other. He told me that he hopes that I could forgive him because he isn't the same person he was then. He was the person I first met, not the person I had an altercation with in my kitchen.

I told him that I was glad that he was doing better and he got the help he needed. I had forgiven TJ a long time before that call and I told him that. He said that he still loves me and if he could change anything that he said or did to me, he would. I told him what happened in the past, is in the past. I dealt with everything and we are ok to live our lives. He is ok to move on and learn from his mistakes. I have moved on and I don't even think about him. He is a part of my past and that will never change, but that is all it will ever be.

The abuse of men and boys is the most pervasive and unaddressed human rights violation on earth

#ViolenceAgainstMen

~~~~~~~~~~~

Remember where you came from but focus on where you are going

~~~~~~~~~~~

Chapter 9

You Are Not Alone

Sometimes when we go through these bouts of abuse, we forget that although we may feel isolated and alone, there are millions of other people in this world going through some of the same situations. You should never walk around with bruises on your body that you have to make excuses for. You should never walk around feeling like you deserved to be abused. Never should you feel less than a worthy, well deserving person who deserves the opportunity to live a positive lifestyle. Your self-esteem is important and you deserve to be happy.

Inside the next few chapters, you will find some stories from fellow abuse victims that have turned a tragic past into a positive future. I hope their stories can help you see the light at the end of the tunnel. I will start this chapter off with Christian's story.

Christian (as told in his words)

*Note – All names have been changed to protect the innocent. If you believe you are being abused in any way, please contact your local law enforcement agency and your local crisis centers or shelters. You can find them in the blue pages of your local phone book. If you are in immediate danger, please find the nearest phone and dial 911.

I want to relate my story, and tell you about how important visualization was for me. I grew up as the child of an alcoholic. Although, I wasn't sexually abused by him, my father's "thing" was to hold us children by the leg or the arm and not let go until we either "lost it" or hit him (which was an excuse for him to give us a whack).

Throughout most of my life, I told myself that compared to some of the things I heard about what other people had to go through, what I experienced wasn't so bad. But, I remember how dis empowered I was and how ineffectual I felt (and how little I valued myself as a result), I couldn't get on with my life. Right up until I had a huge catharsis three years ago. I was stuck in dysfunctional relationship patterns. Even when a good relationship was available, I didn't think I deserved it, so I either avoided it or worse yet, sabotaged it.

There came a point though, when I'd gotten to "the bottom", where I'd f_'d my life up so badly that nothing short of divine inspiration could help me. Somewhere the analogy of an elephant tied to a stake was presented to me. When an elephant is a baby and it's tied by a stake (as I was), it's stuck there because it isn't strong enough to pull it out. When it's bigger (because it's been conditioned by the stake), it doesn't realize it can pull the stake out at any time and be free.

My father was a physically strong man. As I grew up, I tried getting physically bigger and stronger. I pumped iron for hours a day. I looked formidable, but I wasn't spiritually big. To get past my fear and the emotional barriers that I'd adopted (my elephant stakes), I imagined a person outside myself telling their life story (which was actually my life story).

That helped put everything in perspective. I could imagine how they might feel based on what happened to them, what behaviors they might have developed, and what

I would suggest they do to change their life for the better. I was big. I was strong. I changed my life.

Chapter 10

Samantha's Story

Samantha (as told in her own words)

*Note – All names have been changed to protect the innocent. If you believe you are being abused in any way, please contact your local law enforcement agency and your local crisis centers or shelters. You can find them in the blue pages of your local phone book. If you are in immediate danger, please find the nearest phone and dial 911.

   I was the girl next door who grew up in a very loving and beaver cleaver type household. My dad worked hard at the local Westinghouse plant and my mom was a stay at home mom and a very loving one at that.

   I guess the first time I started realizing that there was a "control " issue between my parents was when i was around 14 years old. My mom was sitting on the couch crying and I couldn't help but ask her what was wrong. It was rare that my parents showed any emotions except being happy around us. She said, "I really feel like i would love to have a job, but your dad does not want me to." I remember feeling my first real burst of feminism as I looked at her and said, "Why can't you? We can take care of ourselves now and you should do what you want to do". My mom, being the submissive wife that she was did not want to rock the boat with my dad. I remember feeling furious at my dad for not "allowing" my mom to have some freedom and to get a job because she had to have permission? I mean, give me a break. Why does she have to have his "permission" to have a job? As time went on, I remember my mom confiding in me several more times about this same subject. It definitely gave me a different opinion about my dad, as I was totally disappointed that he was controlling what plans my mom would have. It was then I realized that my dad had a certain control over my mom that was a little on the unhealthy side.

As i went through high school, I remembered my humble Christian upbringing that was so embedded into me. I dated a little in high school, but was more focused on my extra curricular activities than meeting boys and having relationships. Besides, I was supposed to wait until I got married to have sex or to be intimate with a man, so why tempt myself with this so that is why i kept busy in life during that time frame. I was afraid that I would get myself into too much trouble. My lack of dealings with various boys was a precursor to get me into trouble later, as my inexperience would cause me to have some "growing pains " in selecting a proper mate.

I was almost 19 when i met Sam. I had gotten a job at a hardware store with my best friend and as soon as I walked in the place, I noticed a very tall slender guy. I made a comment to my friend, Mary, that I thought he was very good looking. He had the blondish brown hair, blue eyes and had a confidence about him that was alluring.

I had worked at Oscar's hardware for about 3 months or so when I was approached by a guy friend of mine, Bill , to attend a party at his house. I could tell that he kind of had a crush on me, but he was being subtle about it all. After Bill had invited me, Sam walked up and said,"I was going to invite you to my party this same weekend. Don't you want to come to my party? Someone else might want you to come to their party (meaning him)." At that point, I realized that he was interested in me. I was on cloud 9 since I thought he was attractive when I first laid eyes on him. Needless to say, I went to Bill's party one night and Sam's party the next night. After that, Sam and I became closer and really hit it off. We were a couple from that day on.

There were a couple of things that I really liked about Sam. He was very smart, smooth, financially responsible,and what I thought to be a mature guy. I was very attracted to those types , because I still considered myself to be young and impressionable and I felt like I needed someone to guide me through life and help me to find my way. Little did I know that this naivety that I had would lead me to trouble later on.

As Sam and I got to know each other, he would get jealous as I would talk to our guy friends. They would ask me questions and I , of course, would look at them to answer them. He started to pinch my arm when he did not like something I said or did. I noticed this first when I was having dinner at his parent's house. His brother, Bob had turned to me to ask me something and I looked at him and gave him a response. Sam immediately pinched me extremely hard on the arm at the dinner table , where of course, no one could see him do it for me to stop talking to his brother. This was just the beginning of that type of behavior. I later would confront him and he would just say, "Why were you looking at

Bob?" and I would say, "because I was answering his question." and then he would go on a rant about how I was crazy and that it was my problem and not his.

As time went on, this was only the beginning of his controlling behavior. It was almost like I recognized what he was doing, but I always blamed myself and looked at it as being something I did wrong. It was like punishment for me being so lost and naive. The next thing I noticed is that he started to comment on my clothing. I have always had a fashion flair and definitely a style on my own, so I noticed that he was starting to change me into the stepford girlfriend he wanted me to be. I am assuming that the outfits I was wearing was too sexy and over the top for his conservative tastes, so little by little, he started telling me how bad my clothes looked on me and how much better I would look in these very plain clothes that he picked out for me at the mall. I went along with his suggestions, for what did I know, i was young and naive and had no idea what I was doing. I started telling myself that I needed to have someone help me with this. Before I knew it, I was starting to lose my individuality and my own sense of style. He was so convincing that I started to listen to his every word of "advice" .

After a couple of years of dating, he would do things to make me jealous and cause me to act out. There was this girl that he dated previously that kept trying to pop into his life and interfere with our relationship. She also worked with us at Oscar's so that made it much more difficult for our relationships and work situation. It always seemed that he secretly got pleasure out of seeing me squirm. I became infuriated and started to hate the way he made me feel. All of that being said, I still was very invested in this relationship and I figured that I would stick with it, besides, what other guy would have as many "good " qualities as he did? The control issues got worse as our relationship went on. When we would order something or talk to other business people, he would get angry if I gave them my personal information and phone numbers. He then coached me into lying about my phone number because "people don't need to know your personal information". The crazy thing about this was that they did need to know how to contact us and he was controlling me and telling me what to say and even interrupting and adding fictitious information to the people that we were talking with. This infuriated me to no end. We would constantly fight about these type of things because i saw it as necessary info to give and he totally felt the other way. Again, he would act like I was crazy for even going against him. Many times when he would get angry at me, he would pinch my arm really hard or pull me by my arm to let me know that this was not acceptable behavior to him. It got worse and worse. My parents, that I lived with at the time, started asking me about the bruises on my arms. I would make up things to keep them from worrying about me, besides, it was no big deal, right?

Sam had this way of making me beg for his attention. He was not affectionate at all to me. Holding hands and kissing were pretty much non existent. He would always think of ways to with hold any type of affection from me, whether it be because he was mad at something I did, something I said , or because he did not feel like showing affection. As a very affectionate person, this was very hard for me to accept and was a huge sense of rejection for me. Being the overachiever I always was, I was making excuses of why he did not love me the way I thought he should. I started to feel like something was wrong with me and I tried even harder to make him love me. It was emotionally draining for me and through the years, I started to get angry and bitter because I could not seem to get him to cooperate. I was trying so hard with practically the opposite result. He was turned off by my neediness and attempts to capture his attention. Besides, I needed to change myself, right?

About year number 3 or 4, I was sitting on the hood of my car talking to him. Pretty soon the subject about our relationship turned into a verbal argument. Standing in front of me, he got so mad that he pulled back my car antenna and he let go of it angrily. It then hit me in the eye with the tip of the antenna. He went inside to get some ice and then I waited until it got late before I went home so my parents would not know. I could not tell them the truth, as they would definitely have some harsh words about how Sam was treating me. The next morning, I work up and went to work. My eye was extremely sensitive to light and I tried my hardest to work, but people kept asking me why my eye was so red. I made up a story that I hit myself accidentally with the antenna. As the day went on, I started to realize that the throbbing pain was not going away. I went to the urgent care and they immediately sent me to the Baptist Hospital Emergency room . Little did I know that I could have lost sight in that eye if I would not have sought medical help. I ended up in the hospital for 5 days,so I had to stick with my story that i hurt myself, otherwise, my parents would have definitely have had some serious talks with me. I was a big girl and wanted to make my own decisions without my parents butting in. I was definitely very independent yet also stuck in that soul searching time of my life. I was strong and could do this on my own.

The years flew by as I was working full time, school full time and in my spare time was spending time with Sam. Eventually, it came to the point where Sam was jealous and discouraged me in subtle ways to not do things with my friends or either made me feel extremely guilty for going anywhere with my friends. Anything I did that did not revolve around him was frowned upon. It was getting to the point of the 5th and 6th years of dating that I was becoming extremely frustrated , that I felt I was losing my own identity , and that I was not the person that I wanted to be. At my own fault, I had given Sam an ultimatum. We either plan to get married or we go our separate ways. It had been 6 plus years of dating, and I was getting ready to graduate with my bachelor's degree and start my life. I needed to know which way it was headed. We had a huge verbal argument and I had gone to work the next day. He came to my work , flowers in hand begging me to stay in his life. I was at the time, training to be an Assistant Manager for the company that I worked for .

There he was, suckering me back in the many times we had told each other that this was the end of the relationship. We did nothing but argue and I'm not an argumentative person unless provoked. We went back to his parent's house that week and he then told me that we would get married a year after we both graduated from school, at his reluctance. He did not want to get married. I'm not even sure I wanted to get married, but we had been together for so long, that it just seemed like the next step. It was either that or break up. This was the turning point of our relationship. He bought me an engagement ring that I picked out and did not propose to me, rather handed me the box so I could wear the ring and he could claim me as his property. All throughout this process, I questioned myself along the way. I knew I was not happy, however, I had so much invested as far as time and feelings in this relationship that I was terrified to start over, especially since I was in my mid twenties and many people around me (friends and acquaintances) were getting married. I think I was more in love with the planning for the future aspect, rather than getting married. Now, to this day, I tell young ladies that if they want to throw a big life party to get it out of their system, to do so ...and I will help them. I don't want anyone to ever feel the pressure to get married unless that is what they want to do. I think more women are in love with the idea of having a big party in their honor, rather than just getting married so they can have the big party.

A year or so passed by and we were at year number 7. We were planning our wedding and were going to move out together after we got married. After the marriage, I was under his control since he was managing the money. He insisted that I put my paychecks in his account. I had no checkbook of my own. I had to ask for checks so I could grocery shop,etc. I was allowed to spend only $300 a month on my credit card and this included my lunches that I ate for work and any extra stuff I wanted to buy. Let's not go crazy now, wow, a whopping $300 dollars. We were both in management positions with different companies making lots of money, so the hoarding was all because he wanted us to build up our savings account. Nothing wrong with that, however, I could not even argue the point or there would be hell to pay. He would punish me be verbally assaulting me and calling me "stupid" (I think that was his favorite), "Bitch", or "Useless". I had to learn to agree to all his demands or else be very very neglected verbally, emotionally, and in some ways physically. He was very very secretive and expected me to be as well. Because both of our work schedules were not on a regular set schedule, I would ask him what he was working for the week. He would not even tell me that. He would just keep changing the subject or he would yell at me for asking more than once. The only reason I wanted to know his schedule was so I could plan for days off and so I would not worry if he was not home at certain times. My motives were pure and I could not understand what the huge deal is that he would not divulge such a simple thing as his schedule.

Our lives went on and we were both working at least 50 hrs a week at our jobs. Communication was practically non existent between us. We worked opposite schedules most of the time. When we did have a day off, we always had to do what he wanted to do. He was very picky and would not go along the fun things that I usually would suggest. It was as if everything had to be his idea. Mostly, our days off consisted of cleaning the house, cleaning the cars and being anal retentive, basically. He was very OCD/anal retentive and even a simple task as putting the dishes in the dishwasher would turn into a major argument. As soon as I would wipe down the sink, he would come behind me because there were water droplets in the sink and complain endlessly about it. I started to wonder if I was in the military and was undergoing a "white glove " inspection or whether I was a slave under the power of the "master". Resentment was building inside me and I took it as long as I possibly could. There were times he would get so mad at me that he would shove me across the room, yell at me, throw things at me, and the worst actually was the verbal assaults of how useless I was to him. I was trying my best to be perfect, yet, no matter what I did, it was never the right answer and it was never enough.

The next major issue that came up was how long were were going to pay rent and live in that condo that we were living in. I wanted a house, one that I could go outside and sit in my backyard if I wanted to. I wasn't asking for much, just to have a place of our own, a place where I could make it the way I wanted it. It seemed like he was always living as if not wanting to move forward, but to stay where he was comfortable. After 3 or 4 years of looking for houses to build and neighborhoods to build in, he finally decided on a neighborhood that was nice enough and up to his standards. Picking out furniture was extremely interesting, as nothing I picked out was acceptable. We went over and over again to furniture stores looking through the same catalogs to see if they had added a page or what have you. He just could not seem to find anything he liked and far be it from me to have input on this. I only got scolded and scoffed at, so I just gave into his tantrums so there would be peace. As the house was being built, he was constantly arguing with the construction company because things were never up to his standards. No matter what anyone did , it was never right. You would have thought that this man grew up in a family where he got no attention, no love...but the situation was actually quite the opposite. So pretty much all of the decisions for the house were made by Sam. Nothing I suggested was ever satisfactory.

We lived in that house once it was finally built for a year. During that year, Sam and I started to argue more and more. He started staying out late, like around 2 to 3 a.m. in the morning. I would ask him over and over what he was doing and where he was at. He would yell at me and come at me as if he were going to hurt me physically. He refused to answer where he was at or why he was coming home late. I was starting to get physically sick because my life was spinning out of my control. He would push me off the bed so I started to sleep in our guest bedroom so I could sleep soundly. I had a husband that would not talk to me or tell me where he was daily, and I really had no idea what I was going to do. After several months of this behavior and emotional and mental abuse, We finally talked one day . He was so argumentative and out of control that he threw an alarm clock at me and it put about an 8 inch hole in the new sheet rock wall of the house. The alarm clock missed me by only a couple of inches. I demanded that he change, get on some medication, or we would get a divorce. He got on some medication for anxiety and depression and got worse with his behavior.

The staying out late, the verbal attacks, his lack of attention to me it all worsened. I was coming to a breaking point. It was then that I decided to do my own private investigation work. Luckily, I had the cell phones under my name, so I did a search of the phone numbers he had called on his phone. Low and behold, one woman's phone number was on there a couple of times and I started to put 2 and 2 together. He was seeing someone behind my back. One day , I found the keys to his truck (which he hid) and got in his truck while he was in the shower . I found a picture of some woman in his glove box. As I asked him about this, he got more and more enraged and would yell at me. I feared for my safety and then started doing some soul searching.

It was May of 2004 and my birthday was on this day. Not a phone call, not a word from my "husband" was received by me. He made absolutely no effort to recognize my birthday. Not because of the materialistic aspects of my birthday, but because this was the proverbial icing on the cake, that I decided to change my life on that day. I was done with being treated like a stranger, like a useless person, and a person that had no worth. I knew i was a beacon of light and someone that could make a difference in this world, yet my light had been dimmed and almost snuffed out by someone who had learned to control me verbally, emotionally, and physically. My brother had called to wish me a happy birthday and this was an open door for me to spill the beans about my secret life. NO one knew the secrets I kept the secrets of the abuse of which I was suffering. It's as if a light bulb came on that day and I knew I would move forward and never turn back. It took over 3 months for me to get my stuff out of the house and leave and it took me nearly 6 months to get him to sign the divorce papers, but luckily, there were no kids involved, so the divorce went smoothly. I believe he was ready to move on to his life with this new woman anyway and he was just hanging onto me in case that didn't work out.

It is now 5 years later and it seems like a lifetime ago. I spent 14 years of my life with someone who abused and controlled me. It took a good 2 years for me to get over the post traumatic crying and such when I would have flashbacks. I met a wonderful man during the time frame of my divorce that taught me that it was okay to cry and it was okay to work through the sadness. He was the polar opposite of Sam when it came to affection and love. He loved me for me and still does. I'm living proof that a bad situation can become a very positive one. I just would have liked to have recognized it earlier on in my life, but without the life experiences I have had, I would not be the person I am today. I have become a very strong woman with lots of friends and support. I have learned the value of clinging to those people that lift me up and are positive lights in my life and to discard or stay away from those that are negative and that preach a negative lifestyle. I consider myself now a life coach and friend to those who need my strength and light. I feel like I've grown 10 lifetimes since that time of control and sadness. The most important thing that a person needs to realize is to love yourself first and the rest will follow. Believe in yourself , surround yourself with positive influences, and there is no limit as to what you can accomplish and how many people you can help.

From every wound there is a scar, and every scar tells a story. A story that says, "I survived."

Chapter 11

Edward's Story

*Note – All names have been changed to protect the innocent. If you believe you are being abused in any way, please contact your local law enforcement agency and your local crisis centers or shelters. You can find them in the blue pages of your local phone book. **If you are in immediate danger, please find the nearest phone and dial 911.**

Edward (as told in his own words)

I wish I could say the abuse from my father was temporary, but it actually started before I was even born. My mother told me after my father swept her off her feet they were engaged in 6 weeks and married within 6 month from their first date. My mother always wanted to have a baby of her own. She was middle child and not having one of her own really maid the situation urgent for her. My father claiming to want children was more than willing to please his new bride.

From the time they announced that I was on my way my father began to show jealousy. My father wanted my mother's attention and now she was getting attention from both sides of the family and friends about her pregnancy. It did not take long before my mother realized that my father regretted every having me. He would not have anything to do with me at all.

My first real memory of abuse came when I was five years old and I handed my father paperwork from school. I had worked really hard and got a 100 on the work. I remember running up to him to show him and he threw it on the ground saying the he did not want to see this shit,

(Please note that I have vivid memories all the way back to when I was 3 mo. old except for huge blocks of time missing of my father. I believe my mind chose what to and what not to remember as it relates to my father up till the age of five. I am also missing sometime around my younger brother's birth and his first few years. I believe this to be because of sibling rivalry).

My father was illiterate and could not read. I remember him fighting with my mom telling her I was showing off how much smarter I was than him. I remember when my grandfather brought me my first desk for my birthday on Dec. 3. It was the greatest thing in the world. For Christmas I received a huge stand alone chalk board I thought it was the greatest thing in the world.

My joy really sent my father ballistic. The more I enjoyed my things the more he tortured me calling me a sissy boy and then started calling me a girl. He even went as far as to throw all my truck away on day when I was out side playing with them and told me to get in the house because that is where girls belong.

I remember one day I was playing dress up with my mother's cloths with my younger brother and sister while my father was sleeping. When he woke he beat me for try to turn my little brother into a girl like me.

I then remember another time I walked outside to see what everyone was doing, the females had gathered around a shade tree and was talking while the men were working on a car. My little brother was under the hood so walked over and asked to help. My father asked me to grab something from his toll box. I did not now what it was so he grabbed it and beat me with it.

This verbal and physical abuse continued everyday until I was 12 years old. The last beating I took I was attempting to call the police and he grabbed me threw me on the bed and I saw a flash. When I woke up I had to black eyes and a swollen head. He paid me not to report him to the police. Within two month he told us he was leaving because he had been cheating on my mother. I was never so happy in my life.

I ran into the house and grabbed as much of his stuff and threw it out the door. I remember the adults claim I was so mad at him I was acting out. My family began to wonder why I was not upset with him leaving and sent me to therapy. I enjoyed therapy a lot.

I actually learned to play chess in therapy. After about a year the doctor told me I was not going to have to return. I sat in the meeting with my mom and dad when the doctor told me that there was absolutely nothing wrong with me but he recommends that they seek therapy for what had happen to me growing up in the house with my father. Needless to say my father was not happy about what was said.

I was never able to hold a grudge against my mom because she so tried to stop him from hurting me. She did everything humanly possible to buffer me except leaving him. After my father abandoned the family I spoke with my mom about this and she told me that she was sorry. She had two other children to think of and he was not abusive to them. She told me that she prayed every night that he would stop or I would stop coming back at him. My mom told me I was a fighter and I could not be broken.

My father was threatened by me because of my free will and intelligence. I had a mouth on me and even with the threat of beating I would not allow him to control me. It was during these many conversations with my mother she told me that I am not like any person she has ever come in contact with.

As a child I stood strong to my beliefs and in all actuality I brought the worst out in my father just because I was being who I am nothing more or less. It was during this time I realized how much different I was to the actually family I was growing up with.

My family is a blue collar traditional republican family while I am a white collar democrat. I get things done with my brain not with my hands. It was also during this time I began to actually questioned my sexuality and my belief in God. I kept going back to what my therapist kept saying some day soon the world will open up for me and the demographic on the variety of people in this world will be made aware to me.

I started dating my high school friend of two years when I was 17 years old. It was not until I was 20 years old and I was worker with a large diverse employee base I finally had the world open up to me. I met white collar workers who were married with children. I finally realized after this, I am not all that different from most men in the white collar work force. I grew up in a blue collar family while being a white collar person.

I married my high school sweetheart Alison and in 2010 we will celebrate 20 years together. My life after my father left began to change for the better.

As an adult my father continues to disrespect me and my family. I almost have cut all ties with him so not to allow the abusive behavior to affect my wife and children. The affect of the abuse I suffered is being felt more by my brother and sister than me these days.

My father continues to attempt to mentally abuse me after he left up to today. I have not included all the physical and mental abuse I suffered but I think you get the idea. I am a survivor and have hand many successes in my life to help me deal with the abuse I suffered. I credit my father leaving, my mother and my discussion on the abuse, the support of my brother and sister, the love of my life, Sylvia Browne and God.

~~~~~~~~~~~~

Chapter 12

Donatello's Story

*Note – All names have been changed to protect the innocent. If you believe you are being abused in any way, please contact your local law enforcement agency and your local crisis centers or shelters. You can find them in the blue pages of your local phone book. **If you are in immediate danger, please find the nearest phone and dial 911.**

Donatello (as told in his words)

My lovely wife, Alana and I fought a hard, and expensive court battle and managed to win custody of the boys, but only after much damage was done after I divorced their mother. When my sons found that they had to follow the rules, they whined and cried to go back to their overly-permissive mother. Any sort of regimented discipline was not for them, it seems, after they were used to having their way, unsupervised. They made life so difficult for us that we relented. In order to save *this* marriage, I let them have their wish. They were head-strong teenagers by then, and almost totally out of control.

I made a lot of mistakes early on in that marriage. Though I never abused my children in any fashion whatsoever, I was always on the road, trying to "make it" as a musician. When I did see the boys, I made sure to shower them with hugs and love sincere. I think back on their joyous exuberance when I came home from a road trip. Money I sent home was supposed to pay bills and cloth the boys. Yet, when I got home, they were still shabbily dressed and the bills unpaid. However, the boys could tell me where the best restaurants were, and how swell all the movies were, which they went to see every night. They were genuinely happy to see me, though! It still rips at my heart something terrible.

It is strange that I've even had guilt feelings for being brought up in a happy, well-adjusted family. My first wife, on the other hand, came from a terribly abusive environment, and I thought I was "rescuing" her from that. What I failed to realize was that she began exhibiting signs of mental maladjustment early on in the marriage, and became very difficult to live with. ("As the twig is bent, so grows the tree." Walter Russell)

After our first son was born, she all but had nothing to do with me. And I am not 100%

certain that my younger son came from my seed. I wonder about it, after finding out some disturbing things about a man we both knew; a former "friend."

Instead of stepping out of the marriage before the children came along, I stayed, against my better judgment, and in my ignorance, caused much grief for all concerned. My oldest son fared well, and molded himself into a fine character, with no vices and a beautiful, giving soul. My younger son strayed willingly into the dark side and has cut off all communication with me, refusing to return my calls and e-mails. Still, Alana and I are waiting with open arms to welcome him home. When he was seven, he told Alana, "I wish *you* were my mother."

I am not blameless through all of this. And I have agonized and suffered untold sorrow because of not knowing what the hell I was doing. I did not have the courage to say no to marrying at too young an age, before I had a chance to find out who I am, and follow my dream of a life in one of the most unstable careers ever; the music business.

I have learned much and have grown a lot in knowledge and character, in spite of myself. I have found great joy in my twenty-five-year marriage to the most wonderful woman I could ever hope to meet. Trying to undo all the damage I caused, by turning it around, replacing it with the giving of unselfish Love, has been my quest for the remainder of my life.

Strength does not come from physical capacity. It comes from an indomitable will.

~GANDHI

Chapter 13

Briana's Story

*Note – All names have been changed to protect the innocent. If you believe you are being abused in any way, please contact your local law enforcement agency and your local crisis centers or shelters. You can find them in the blue pages of your local phone book. **If you are in immediate danger, please find the nearest phone and dial 911.**

Briana (As told in her own words.)

My story of abuse is one not usually detected by others, but is abuse nonetheless. I was the normal teenager growing up, but got pregnant at seventeen. The father and I decided that we would get married right after I graduated and the baby was born. Things with him seemed ok, but really there were signs that I over looked and that should have sent up red flags. Of course I thought I loved him so it was easy to overlook.

I remember the first time I was caught off guard by his temper. I was in my second trimester and we had gotten into an argument. Me being bull headed, was not about to back down. He became very angry and then pushed me as hard as he could which landed me on the bed. This doesn't seem very important, but in reality he had no right to even touch me or to take out any aggression on me in any way like that.

He had done this only a few times, while I was pregnant. I had indeed graduated and only a few short weeks later, my baby was born. Things seemed pretty quiet or so I thought and I thought it wouldn't happen anymore. It was a month later when we got married, and it was then that it had started again, but seemed to morph into something more.

My baby boy had been sleeping in his crib and once again we had an argument. Now I considered these issues to be pretty petty, but as a teen or a young couple, they can seem larger than life. As the argument grew, so did his temper. Before I knew it, he had me by the throat, pinned to the floor. It was then that I heard my one month old baby boy scream a blood-curdling cry like I had never heard before. It was then that he had let me go. I believe to this day, that my son knew something was wrong and with out hearing what was going on, he instinctively knew and felt what was going on around. Never let you think that your kids don't know what is going on around them. They are smarter than we give them credit for.

Over the next two years, he continued to "black out" as he called it and began to hit me in places where others wouldn't see then marks. Several times I had softball size bruises on my legs. Another time he slammed my head against a cement wall.

Even from the beginning he would commit the crime, profess his love, apologies, offer to turn himself into the police, and say he would never do it again. Each time it was just a hollow expression to cover his temper and hope that I would not leave him.

He finally messed up and choked me in front of someone. This occasion was a strange one and out of character for him as he was usually very careful. We were just wrestling around having fun ,but all of a sudden he pinned me down by the throat and started choking me. My good friend was there and saw it all happen. He told him to let me go, but he didn't. It was then that he felt exactly what it felt like to be pinned down by the throat. I took my exit from the room, and so did my friend. My husband sat there and sulked ad became very angry at the fact that I didn't go in there to see if he was ok. Well, why should I? This was when I had made the decision that enough was enough.

Over the next few weeks, I had made strategic plans to get rid of him so that I could move on with my life. I had already lost two years of my life, and put my son's mental state and well being in jeopardy over this jerk.

I had made arraignments to move out of my parents house and got lucky enough to move into an apartment above my best friend and her husband. This would ensure I had someone who knew what was going on near me and would in fact hear me yell if I needed them.

Once I had moved out, I had made sure that my guy friend (the same one that had physically defended me before) stay the night and that I decided to break it off with my husband so that if something were to happen I actually had someone in the same house with me.

It worked and he left even thought he didn't leave my life completely due to us having a child together. Unfortunately even now, 18 years later, he hasn't changed and even though has has never hurt our son physically, he played head games with him his whole life. Fortunately, it was finally this summer (2009) that my son seen his father for the person he is and has now vowed to never speak to him again. If he does or not is up to him, but I am pretty sure it will at least be a very long time. Oh and he friend that defended me, we have been happily married for 14 years.

~~~~~~~~~~~~~

The scars don't define you but they make you stronger

~Unknown

CHAPTER 14

How Your Loved Ones Cope

Sometimes, when we go through tough times, we forget that we are not the only ones handling the emotional effects. When you hurt, your family and friends are also hurting. When you think you are all alone where no where to turn, it is your loved ones that are sitting there dealing with the hurt of watching you endure the abuse.

We, as humans have our own reasons why we choose to stay in our abusive situations. We give excuses for everything in life and staying in an abusive situation is no different. We don't want to break up the family or think we can't get anyone better in our lives. The truth is that your family and friends are there for you and they are going through emotions of their own such as feeling useless and unable to help.

Even if you think you don't need the help, you really do. Your loved ones are looking at the situation from an outsider's perspective. They are not emotionally attached to your partner as you are. Sometimes when you are in a relationship, it is hard for you to see things from a different perspective because you are emotionally involved. Listen to your family and friends and try to see things from their point of view then make your decision on how things should change.

Below are stories from people who have witnessed their loved ones in abusive relationships. They are trying to give you examples of how your loved ones may be going through YOUR abusive relationships. You will be looking at these stories as an outsider. What would you do in each situation? What advice would you offer the victims of these situations? What advice would you give to the family and friends of the victims. Oh and by the way, the loved ones are also victims in this. Now take how these stories make you feel. Get an idea of how your family and friends feel and try to apply that to your situations.

~~~~~~~~~

Alice's Family Story (as told in her words)

*Note – All names have been changed to protect the innocent. If you believe you are being abused in any way, please contact your local law enforcement agency and your local crisis centers or shelters. You can find them in the blue pages of your local phone book. **If you are in immediate danger, please find the nearest phone and dial 911.**

This story is about my identical twin sister. Karen was a fun loving free spirit, full of life, funny gregarious personality, full of style and confidence. Karen was always happy, looked great, wore great looking clothes, hair done, makeup, lots of jewelry, etc. Mind you, she was not the most disciplined of young ladies when it came to domestic chores so when her new husband Frank began showing controlling behaviors and being disapproving of her, Karen chalked it up to him being "very particular" in the way he likes things done. This came as such a surprise to Karen because she said Frank was not like that during their courtship and had been such a gentleman.

My first observations of Frank's behavior was when I saw him with Karen's daughter Lisa sitting at the dinner table during a visit. Lisa is Karen's daughter from a previous marriage and was about 7 at the time. She was not wanting to eat, saying she did not like any of the food. Where this may be a normal challenge for parents, Frank's level of belittling and controlling was disturbing. The way Frank seemed to delight in Lisa crying was most upsetting to me. The more she sat at the table crying, the bigger his smile got all the while looking over at the family as if to say, "Look at me, I can break her." At the same visit I saw Frank constantly tearing Karen down about everything and making her the butt of his jokes. I kept looking at him sternly saying little things to him about it, but it was obvious he considered me "just like her" and brushed off any comments I made.

Over the following years, Karen constantly complained to our family about Frank's behavior toward her. It was very frustrating for us because Karen would be so upset when she told us things he did but as soon as we tried to get her to get out of the situation or take a stand she would in turn get mad at our response and start defending him. This cycle continued with only brief periods of quiet. Karen lived in a different state which only added to the family's worry that we couldn't just pop in to see if everything was ok.

Ten years into their marriage, Karen gave birth to their son, Joseph, That is when everything seemed to take a turn for the worse. Frank began obsessing over his son Joseph. He would do everything for Joseph and not allow Karen to be a normal mother. Over time, Frank took all parenting responsibilities from Karen including going to the school, after school activities, cooking, everything. Karen was being made a bystander in her own house, and not being allowed to mother her son. By this time Lisa had grown and moved on to college so it was just Karen, Frank, and Joseph in the household. What surprised our family the most was that Karen did not seem to have the desire to fight back or stand up to Frank taking over like this and would disregard any concerns we expressed.

As their son Joseph grew, he grew with the upbringing that his mother was an idiot and did not know how to do anything. Joseph now treats his mother the same way he saw his father treat her. Karen told me there isn't a day that goes by Frank and Joseph don't call her an idiot, fat or stupid. Again, Karen would complain about it to us but not do anything to remedy the situation. I even tried sending Karen some cash to stow away in case she needed emergency money only to find that she handed it over promptly to Frank.

Karen's daughter Lisa now talks openly about Frank and the way he is so emotionally abusive to her mother. Lisa despises Frank but loves her brother Joseph and realizes he is only copying his father's behavior. Lisa seems angry with her mother for staying in such a marriage. Lisa relays that she begged Karen to leave Frank early on in their marriage but said Karen told her she did not want to leave Frank because he would take good financial care of them.

Twenty one years later, the emotional control and abuse have taken their toll. Karen is no longer a vibrant, outgoing woman who was once the Manager of a Travel Agency. She is now a meek, lowly, quiet and totally passive individual. She does not dress up anymore, fix her hair or wear make-up like she used to. Her personality has totally changed. Karen is not allowed to have any money, drive a car, or work. She is not allowed to know anything about their finances. Karen is not allowed to cook, wash clothes or do any of the normal motherly duties that one could take pride in. Karen does not even know what school her son Joseph attends. She is not allowed to ask questions without verbal repercussions. She is not allowed to use the internet or make long distance phone calls including calling her family. Karen no longer shows any interest in us or her daughter Lisa and has not even tried to see her new grandson.

In addition, there is now something medically wrong with Karen. Karen's memory is incredibly bad, she cannot do simple math, she sees people who are not there on occasion and you can hardly talk to her because she has such trouble searching for words. I have spoken to Frank several times in the last year about Karen seeing a Doctor and he refuses. The last conversation I had with Frank, I asked him why he was not concerned about Karen's well being and he told me to "kiss his ass" and hung up.

I was successful last year getting Frank to allow Karen to come stay with me for 3 months by paying all expenses. Frank agreed because he said he and Joseph were going through hell with Karen's inadequacies and they could use a break. When Karen was with me, I got her hair done, helped her put on makeup, took her out to enjoy life, and did as much as I could do for her. I tried to get her medical help and offered to pay for it, but she refused saying that Frank would disapprove if she went without him. I tried on a daily basis to convince her to leave him but to no avail. It was so discouraging for me because when I put her on the plane to go back to him she looked so good and was starting to get some of her confidence back. I sometimes lie in bed at night thinking about how much I hate this man who took my dearly beloved twin sister and turned her into this. In my mind his actions are nothing short of attempted murder. Even though Frank was not physically abusive to Karen, he hurt something far worse than her body, he hurt her spirit.

After she went back home, I rallied family support to get Karen some kind of help. We contacted an attorney who told us we could do a lot to help her including petition the court for Guardianship of her. But the caveat is...Karen has to want the help and agree for us to intervene. **Karen will not**! She does not want to break up her family or leave Frank. As far as the family goes, whenever Karen relays something bad Frank had said or done, we all respond that she deserves better and should leave him. We have told Karen that all she ever needs to do is give us a call and we will come running to help. We have offered any support that we can feasibly give and continually tell her that his behavior is causing harm and damage.

When I asked Karen why she would not consider leaving this abusive relationship she once told me if she did, Frank would surely turn his verbal and emotionally abusive behavior on Joseph. Karen says Joseph would never leave his father to go with her and Karen feels she needs to be there to absorb the abuse and protect Joseph as she had Lisa. This mind set is so very upsetting for us as her family because we know she will be just fine without him and finally have the opportunity for a happy fulfilling life.

I am telling this story to show our family's pain and the struggle families go through when their loved ones are in an abusive relationship. It is not just the person who is being abused that suffers. Every day I think of Karen, and I feel so guilty living a happy life knowing that my identical twin is living such a miserable one.

I will always continue to try some how, some way to get through to Karen and help her. To this end, I hope my story helps someone else who is being abused to see

that their actions of staying in the relationship and not getting out or getting help not only hurt themselves, but the family around them as well.

~~~~~~~~~

"How you live your life doesn't always only affect you. You have family and friends that you mean everything to. Listen to them as they listen to you"

~ Stacy Lupinacci

How My Mother's Abusive Relationship Affected Me

I am including another one of my stories in this book, although this is going to be the much shorter version of what actually happened. The whole story may become another book. Who knows what the future holds? This is my perspective of my own mother's abusive relationship.

My mother met George when I was around eight years old. There was always drinking involved for as long as I can remember. I remember coming home from school one day, Valentine's Day, and hearing that my mother and George had gotten married. There was a party going on. My mother looked happy but I'm not sure that any of us had any idea of how life was going to be.

In May of 1986, both my brother and I were removed from the home and placed in foster care. George was not allowed to visit us at first. The drinking had to stop and George had to work on himself. There were strict rules on how and when, he was going to be able to take part in any visitations with us. Did that ever come to pass? I'll explain a little more in a bit.

George was able to visit with us after a while when the state thought that the rules was being followed and everyone was doing what they were supposed to be doing. There would be home visits by the state before any visitations could take place at home. Both my mother and George were able to have us visit their home. As much as I loved my foster parents at the time, my mother was my mother and I wanted to come home. Little did I know what all I was moving into.

In 1989, I moved back with my mother and George. I was told that they were going to have a beer to celebrate me coming home. What was one beer each? I can tell you what that meant. Some things never changed. One beer turned into two and that night turned into every night. I brought to their attention that they had said that they were going to drink that night to celebrate me coming home. That same excuse was used when my brother came home. That was more proof that things didn't change but cover ups were used to make people think that situations had changed.

George started off calm but then little things would set his temper off and once he got to drinking too much, he would then start physically attacking my mother. I can not begin to tell you how many times I had to jump in the middle or start yelling that he stop assaulting my mother. He didn't care either. He didn't care who was around. If he told my mother to do something and she said no, that would set him off.

One night, he got so drunk that he tried to throw my kitten, Frisky, because he was mad at me. I jumped off of the couch and grabbed my cat. He got mad because I got in front of him and grabbed my cat while trying pushing him back. He let go of the cat and started choking me. I was able to kick him off me and I left the house.

I severely despised George. It wasn't bad enough that he was physically assaulting my mother, but now he is going to take his anger out on myself and my pet. I prayed that he would disappear. There were plenty of times that the police were called and trips to the ER because of his antics. There were plenty of school days that I missed because I was up late because of my mother and George fighting.

Witnessing my mother being abused, took its toll on me. There was one night, I just couldn't take it anymore. I hated that I couldn't stop him from attacking my mother and I hated that she wouldn't leave him. I was fed up. Around the corner from my house was a park. I left and walked to the park and just sat up in one of the play structures, contemplating on what I was going to do. I hated living in that house! I wanted out. What could I possibly do?

Then I heard what I thought was the answer to all of my problems. This could be the answer that I've been waiting for. This could release everything and make it so I don't have to deal with my living situation any more.

I saw a vehicle coming across the parking lot and I knew who it was. I didn't want to go home and I was fed up with everything. I heard the sound of an oncoming train just on the other side of the fence. As the train approached, I ran for the fence bound to jump in front of the oncoming train. It was the only way I could see ending having to witness my mother being physically attacked night after night. Just as I was going to jump the fence, an arm grabbed me and pulled me away from the fence. If I were to jump the fence, there would have been no way to avoid the train. The fence was that close to the tracks. The distance across the tracks was the width of the train, plus a foot or two. There was no way I was going to live through that. At the time, I thought it was best. Now I know better.

Today, I look back and I thank anyone and everyone that was responsible for that intervention. I was 14 years old and to look back at everything I have gone through, I am glad that those events happened. I have learned to deal with life 1000% better. The sad part is that not everyone can,and you as the victim, may not understand the depths of emotions that your loved ones are going through over your abuse.

We ended up moving into a motel because, to some, the beer was more important than paying rent. The drinking never stopped and the fighting was continuous. My mother would go to work the next day with bruises. I hated having to make sure that she was ok. I had to witness the abuse that my mother endured and no matter what was said to her, she was stuck in the middle. Like most abusive relationships, she was being controlled and I hated it.

I had gotten another kitten when we lived in the motel. George got mad one day because I wouldn't do something he said and threatened to throw my kitten over the balcony. I told him, no he wasn't and when he grabbed the carrier that my kitten was in, I grabbed him and started attacking him. He pushed me back and luckily there was someone there to get in the middle. He tried to grab the cat and I told the other person to not let him touch my cat. If it wasn't for that person, someone was getting hurt that day. George did in fact use his brain that day and knew to not raise his hand to the other person. Personally I wish he did. I'm sure he would have seen what it was like to get slapped around. He would have deserved it.

Night after night, my mother would get hit for something. It didn't even have to be anything she did or didn't do. She could have been sitting there and because he was mad and wanted a punching bag, she would get it. I hated it. I vowed to never allow myself to be in that kind of relationship. I ended up being in one relationship that ended in a physically abusive way, but that was the only one. I even forgave once or twice, both with cheating and physical abuse. In the end, it had to end. It did end.

CHAPTER 15

Positive and Spiritual Recovery

I have been asked, how do I make a positive outcome to a horrific and devastating situation. There is no one correct answer that fits everyone's situation. We are living in a realm where we, as humans have grown up conditioned to a certain way of thinking. Society, in general has been brought up to believe in this physical world and anything that is not in black and white, doesn't exist. To those, there is no grey.

Do you ever ask yourself, how can you forgive someone that has done you wrong? Have you ever wondered why people tell you that it is important to forgive people who have brought negative actions and thoughts to you? Well the reason for that has nothing to do with them. It is all about you.

That's right! It's about you. We can create good and bad in our lives. What we do is not who we are. You have to forgive because when you don't forgive, you are giving that person or people a power to hold over you. You are giving them the power to control your life. They will control how you interact with people in general. They will control how you interact with your loved ones in your romantic relationships. You end up making excuses to sabotage everything in your life, if you don't realize it. You need to take that power back. Live your life the way YOU want to live it. Not the way someone else is making you live it.

Ultimately, you can be your own worst enemy. When the abuser is gone, it is time for you to work on yourself. Don't be stubborn or allow your pride to get in the way of your healing process. If you need counseling, get it. If you feel better talking with peers who have gone through the same thing, join a group counseling session. There are people that are out there to help you, no matter who you are. It's never easy to separate ourselves from the emotional and abusive attachment we have with the abuser.

You are carrying the negativity within you and are capable of projecting that negativity onto others. It's ok to acknowledge the negativity, but you have to release the negative and surround yourself with positive people and positive actions. The healing process is a very lengthy process and there is no quick fix on getting through the recovery of what has happened to you. Healing must be start on a soul level. You can not just wish it away. You can not just push every emotion and thought under the rug to go away. Even is you put it in the back of your mind, it is still going to be there and there are always little triggers to bring those emotions to the surface if they are not dealt with properly. Eventually, you WILL have to deal with it. It will affect everything you do in your life, this one and the next. (yes I believe in past lives, but that is another story for another day.)

Start doing what people call, soul searching. Really look deeply within yourself and see the beautiful you, the real you. Do not allow what you have gone though take control and ruin your life. Cleanse yourself from all of the regret of believing it was your fault, that you could have changed it, or for some reason you deserved it. These are all natural and normal reactions, but you can change it.

There is an old saying that misery loves company, but you don't have to be that company, even if it's just on a spiritual level. You do not have to allow people to surround you with the negativity in their lives. That includes them treating you with negativity. No matter what anyone says, you have the power to make your future. You have the power to make your own tragic past into a positive future.

It is like the saying, it isn't what people call you, it's what you answer to. It isn't what people have done to you, it's how you take that experience and move on to a brighter future. Know that you deserve happiness and you deserve to not have the negativity that occurs to you, affect the way you live your life. Know that you, yourself is not responsible for what happened to you. The abusers will tell you anything to lower your self-esteem, self-worth, and your own confidence. Never let what others say bring you down. Keep your head up, walk with pride that you made it through, and know that you are worthy to those that deserve you.

We sometimes take on the guilt due to what our abusers say to us. Know that it isn't your fault. This is a life experience that you are working through. It may still be happening to you and you not even realize that it's going on. We, unbeknownst to ourselves, let those that hurt us keep that emotional hold over us. That is in fact what they want. They want us to want them. They want us to feel that we can not get any better. The pain we allow ourselves to hold on to will make us physically as well as mentally sick. It is up to you to not let them have that hold on you.

We also allow those people to affect how we treat future relationships. Know that not everyone is out to hurt you physically or emotionally. Take what has happened to you and turn that negative energy and turn it into something positive. Write A LOT!!! If you feel that you can't talk to someone, write it down.

Don't take the negativity of your past out on the positive of your future.

I have been asked, "Well, what about your parents? Where were they? Why or how did they allow this to happen to you? These are all questions I, myself would have been asking, had I been on the other side of the conversation. Since I am on the abused side of the conversation, I can look back and see how they didn't see anything happening.

My parents were both heavy drinkers when I was growing up. This is not an excuse, but looking back, as I am now older I can see that there were bad choices that both of my parents made that I don't agree with, but I can say that we were loved. Some people would say that they were bad parents. I do not see them as bad parents, but rather people who made some bad choices. To their defense though, I must say that when a person is being abused, they tend to be able to hide the abuse. Victims of abuse can put up a wall like no one else to portray a life to those around them for their own safety as well as the safety of their loved ones.

I know I sometimes build a wall around me to deal with what I am going through on a daily basis so no one would know. I think there are still times even today where I start building the wall when I want my alone time and no one to see how I truly feel about things. I also know that I built a wall around me then to deal with everything I was going through then. We didn't have what other children had, materialistically, but our parents worked hard to provide a home for us and loved us just the same.

I am a firm believer that we write our own charts of events and experiences to have while we are here on earth. With that being said, it is sometimes hard for us to think that we wrote for some of these tragic events to happen. For me, these events have been learning experiences to learn from and advance spiritually.

I realize it is hard for everyone to understand my concepts that I just stated above, but I really believe that once we look at everything with a different perspective, it helps us to understand things a little differently. It gives us a chance to think of things more of a spiritual experience to learn rather than a physical one just because someone wasn't watching out for us.

Sometimes, our physical, human, and conscious minds take over and we find ourselves hating and holding grudges against those that have done us wrong. I can honestly understand. I, myself have done this and sometimes continue to. It is not easy to recover from events such as those mentioned in this book, but it is possible and it is important to do so. I sometimes have to stop myself and think. Yes I get mad and upset with people who are negative or perform negative acts to me. That I can't deny, but I also allow myself to feel the emotions and then I force myself to move on. There is no reason to live in the past. It is what it is and what is done is done. You can't change the past, but you can shape your future.

When we make amends with ourselves, we can move on to heal. We sometimes blame ourselves for the things that happen to us. We need to realize that these tragic events we endure were not our fault. There events were not meant to hinder us, but meant to help us experience, learn, and grow. We can learn from these experiences and help others do the same. All of us are connected by similar events. All of us can help each other as well as other victims get through it. We tend to think we are alone. You are never alone.

Some of us have experienced abuse much worse than others. Some of us have experienced much less violent experiences. It doesn't matter. We are all one. Sometimes, we all need to be reminded of just how special we all are. It doesn't matter what kind of abuse you have encountered or by whom. It could be abuse of ANY kind from a parent to a romantic relationship with a loved one, or even from a stranger. Abuse is abuse!

Forgive someone for the wrong they have done to you and then forgive yourself for any negativity you thought onto yourself or them. Forgiving yourself on a spiritual level will lead you to a spiritual recovery and allow you to help others do the same. This is where the true healing begins.

The physical bruises and pain will go away. It's not hard to hide from the physical pain. The hard part is hiding from the emotional and spiritual elements that come with abuse. It take a person a lot of will power and the want to heal emotionally and spiritually.

You will never forget what happened, no matter how hard you try. Believe it or not, that is a good thing because then we never forget our lessons that have made us stronger. We can not control what people say and do to us, but we can control how we react to it. You are a victim, but you don't have to play the victim role. You don't have to make yourself out to be the innocent and helpless victim that everyone should have pity and feel sorry for. I may get some feedback from that last comment, but it's ok. It is the truth. If you don't know how to take the control back of your life, partner up with someone that does. I have personally talked to as well as know those that play that part. This is not a way of living, but I know people that actually like playing the victim role because they have said when people think of you in the victim role, you get more help from others. Seriously, that is what I have been told by a couple of people and all I could do was look at them and shake my head before going into a deeper conversation with them.

When you are a victim, you have the power to change the world right at your fingertips. You, of course have to heal yourself first. That's the most important thing to do. Allow yourself to feel every emotion that comes to you, but then grab those by the horns and show them that they are not who you are. Once you gain honest control of yourself, then you can talk with other victims while empathizing and sympathizing with them. In my personal opinion, it is easier to talk to other people who have gone through similar experiences, rather then someone who they feel wouldn't know how they actually feel because they, themselves have never had to deal with a situation like yours. Even though that last statement is my own personal opinion for personal reasons, it is also very important to talk to anyone about what has happened to you.

There are numerous outlets to assist you in your healing process. These outlets allow you to process what has happened and be able to lead yourself to a healthy recovery. We as humans, sometimes think we can handle everything and anything. As true as it is that we all handle things our own way, we sometimes forget to ask AND accept help while we recover.

Talk about your experiences. You are going to hurt, cry, be mad, confused, and any other kind of emotion possible. These are normal and healthy responses to the tragic events that you have experienced.

Meditation is a wonderful and spiritual (not to be confused with religious) practice which benefits everyone. Everyone should meditate, even if you have not experienced anything tragic. It's a wonderful tool to manage stress and spiritually cleanse yourself of any negativity (not to be confused for demons or anything like that).

You could and should use affirmations and mantras everyday. These are phrases and groups of words that are positive and will help you really value yourself. You are a valued, beautiful, and blessed person and you should see yourself as such. Look in the mirror everyday and without hesitating you can say the following:

- "I am beautiful/handsome. I am worthy of being loved. I love myself and no one can change that."
- "I love myself for the wonderful spirit I am."
- "I know I am a bright light in a sometimes dark world. Let my bright light shine for all to see. (trust me they will)

You can't lie to yourself. You might not feel any of the above is true. You may not even want to believe it at first, but trust me, you deserve all of the positive and wonderful things this world has to offer. You deserve the abundance of love and to be loved. No one has to live out their life, scared of the next person. Especially if that new person is a loved one. Not everyone is going to treat you the same way you have been treated in the past. Don't make your future pay for your past.

My Own Personal Growth Over the Years

Today I often get asked a lot how I can be so positive with everything I have gone through. How am I not angry while holding grudges? The truth is I was very angry for many years up until my late teens. At 19 years old I started having a specific recurring dream that continued for 3 days. I literally could not sleep for the 3 days this dream kept recurring. Finally one of my best friends helped me figure out the dream. At that point, I started meditating and listening to my inner voices as they started to guide me to reevaluating my life. At this age I also heard someone say, "Forgive them, not for them but for you. Holding on to the anger allows them to keep the control over your life." This was a very pivotal point in my life.

I have always wanted to grow up and have control over as much of my own life as I could possibly have. Being young I wasn't able to do what I wanted. My words meant nothing to so many. Kids were to be seen and not heard. No matter what I said or did, there was always someone who led me to believe my words were not important. Evidence proved them right. Being young and experiencing many of the events I have, led me to who I am today.

I have no regrets. When I tell people this, I always get the usual response, "Yeah right. You must regret something in your life?" The truth is, no I don't. I have come to realize Every event I have had in my life has made me who I am today. Every person I have met, has help develop me into the person I have become and has also helped me learn how to coexist with other human beings. I am good at blending in with my surroundings and in order to do it, I have been able to read people according to their energy as well as their actions.

I understand that no matter what I have gone through, I am not responsible for any events in my life. As a child, you can not accept the blame for what people make you listen to. Their negative energy is theirs to endure. As an adult when you go through events similar to those in previous stories, know that no is no. You are able to say no without the expectation of having to complete any unwanted requests.

Know that you can come back from the negativity your mind as convinced you was the truth. When you hold on to the anger you allow those who hurt you to keep control over your mind and body. When you continue to see yourself as a victim, again they are holding the key to your happiness. If you find that you are not able release the negative thoughts, please find the help you need. It is ok to feel down and defeated. You are not alone. Many have done so .

I had to learn to listen to myself and not what others thought about my thoughts. That may sound weird but think about it. When you put your thoughts out there whether it be you writing a book, journaling, podcast, or just voicing your opinion in a conversation, people will either agree or disagree with you. Some of your thoughts and opinions may be something that is personal to you and / or they may not want to understand where you are coming from. You need to stay true to your thoughts and not let others sway you from your feelings and beliefs.

I know what is wrong and right but sometimes people will make you feel crazy because they don't want your knowledge of the truth to be heard. I had to understand that as long as I am being truthful, I had to not let others opinion and the want to fit in and be heard change my thoughts just to please those who didn't agree with me.

The real truth is, even with all of this knowledge, I still had some residual effects from my past. In some cases, I still do. Again, I'm not perfect. I am a human being with real emotions, even though I don't like to show them and have often used sarcasm, irritation and at times anger to mask how my mind and body was dealing with those in my life. I did drugs and drank to hide my feelings of everyday dealings of life. I worked all hours having multiple jobs to keep busy. I would keep the smile on my face to keep those wondering.

I had to remember that not everyone is out to hurt me. I used to <u>hate</u> when I walked down and people, mainly guys would look at me. I always got an attitude with them and always told them to take a picture because it would last longer. It always made me feel uneasy like they were also going to try and take me as the others have.

One day a friend was walking with me and upon us walking past a group of guys who looked at us, she saw how I reacted. It was then she said, "Why get so mad when guys look at you? You are beautiful! Embrace that." I didn't want to hear it at first but this was part of me processing how I wanted to live my life and what I was willing to let upset me for what was very likely no reason except for me to keep my guard up as a result for my past. It was then I decided to not care about the small things in life that I can not control including who looks at me as a start.

It isn't always easy to adapt to the world around me when I have to wear many hats. I have worked through me experiences and opened my mind to how people interact with each other. "People watching" helps me to understand how and sometimes why people do what they do. I just remember that I can not control what others do and say, including towards me but I can and will control what I allow them to say and do as well as how I react.

It isn't about what you went through and got knocked down but how you got back up and took control over your own happiness. It is about your journey and how you changed your mindset and finally saw you were worth more than any diamond. You are a beautiful soul whether you are a man or a woman and not one who puts you through any continuous tragic event deserves the light you were meant to emit. Just don't allow someone to consume space in your head rent free. It is too expensive to allow someone to consume your mind at your expense.

You are the epitome of love and

self worth. No one can take those

values away from you. Only you

can give them up. Make sure you

give them only to those that

deserve them.

~Stacy Lupinacci

Women who abuse men brainwash their partner to believe that he is not manly (or whatever word she uses to diminish him). Then society tells him he is unmanly to admit his partner abuses him. Is it any wonder men choose to silently suffer instead of getting the support they need to leave

~ Unknown

CHAPTER 16

Not All Abusers Are Men

This is a story from one of my own sisters. She had a wild life that has led to her herself being abuse. In turn, she had become the abuser. Now the fact that she was abused doesn't give her the right to abuse, and luckily she is attempting to overcome some of those wild ways. My sister still battles some of those proverbial "demons" within, but every day is a process that hopefully, she is willing to take and work on.

Now she is a grown adult who has regrets about how she has lived her life. We should have regrets but only to a degree depending on the situation. It's ok to feel bad about what you have done, but also know that this life is a learning lesson for everyone.

It takes a bigger person to admit their faults and work on changing things for the better. There are plenty of other ways a person can abuse themselves as well as others. I just hope EVERYONE in the situation can change for the better and STOP THE ABUSE!!! This is truly a reminder that not all men are the ones doing the abusing.

~~~~~~~~~~~~~~~~

I have had so much abuse in my life. I have been abused, but I have abused just as many. I'm trying to make things right with everyone.

Those who I have abused physically as well as mentally includes, but not limited to, my mom, sisters, friends, and for the most part, my husbands (I have been married 4 times). They did not deserve it but alcohol and drugs have had a huge impact on mine and what I have done. This is no excuse for anything.

When you love someone, you do not let them know by control. I totally believe in karma. What you give out, you get back. I have done a lot of abusive things. Members of my family have been raped and assaulted as well as mentally abused. I could have stopped my sister's abuse, but I was too worried about me and partying.

Thank God I have made things right with people for the most part. I still have to work on some forgiveness issues.

My biological son is emotionally abusive at times and I blame that on me. He saw a lot, heard a lot and had a rough life. I pray that he is able to find the good in himself and let go of the negativity.

My daughters have been terribly abused and they still do, but they try to hide the fact that abuse is happening. This is something I try to get them to open up about. I myself have hidden a lot of things about abuse and have tried to not let others know.

People think they can hide abuse but you can not. Even some of the greatest people in the world can be abused and/or abusive. My mom always did and it hurt so bad to hear her crying from being physically assaulted by her ex-husband. We are all guilty of the same thing. We put up with what we have to.

I have to give people credit when they decide to get out and get their lives straightened out for the most part. It takes a lot of courage and strength. I applaud those that do it.

I have a lot of physical and mental issues now and I hate what I did to so many people. I wish I had realized a long time ago, but I do now. To those people that I have done wrong, I truly apologize. Those people know who they are. Stacy, I love you with all my heart and always will be. I am so proud of you and the woman you have become.

People think that women, just women get abused. They are not the only ones. Women do it to men also. I know that I have physically as well as mentally abused men.

My mom always told me that I would have worse problems with my children. I sure know now how she felt with me. I have shed a lot of tears over my children. They are grown now and I pray to God that they make it through ok. My 9 grandchildren are not abusive but it's hard to predict the future for anyone. While you are healing, help someone else. Life is too short for the hurt, the pain, and the hatred.

I am 41 years old and I wish I could make things right with everyone but it's too late for some. Some of those people I have loved and abused and can never try to fix it in person. I can just say it to God and he will let them know. I love and miss so many people and apologize to the ones I can. However it maybe done. Everyone stay strong and let the ones you love know how much they mean to you and regret what you have put them through.

God Bless You All!

Chapter 17

A Note To Abusers

I am not concerned whether you are a man or a woman. If you are abusing someone, no matter what form of abuse it is, you <u>must</u> stop what you are doing. What you are doing is morally and in most cases, legally wrong.

There is an area within us where the core of our essence is located. We are spiritual beings having a human experience. For us as humans, this is a very hard concept to accept. We have an abundance of human traits and we have a hard time accepting them. One of the main concepts we have is accepting our actions as our own.

We as humans need to accept our actions as our own responsibilities and stop putting the blame on everyone else. Accept the actions you created whether they are good or bad. The things we create are reflections of how we think we are or how we see ourselves. We can all create good and we can all create bad. What we do is not who we are.

Think of the following before the next time you decide to attack someone:

- Do I really have to abuse someone to prove I love them?
- Am I really being a good partner if I try to control and abuse someone?
- Would you want your children growing up thinking this is ok and the right live to live?
- How would you feel if your child or parent were to come home and tell you that they are being abused?
- If you learned this behavior, you can unlearn it!

All abusers, have their own personal issues that must be addressed. You are not capable of properly loving someone if you have not addressed your own emotions and realities. The person you choose to abuse can not help you. They can not make you a better person. You need to take that responsibility and chose to change your life. You as the abuser, never want to admit that it is YOUR fault that you abuse. It is not your parents, it is not your siblings or your friends. It is yours. No matter what you have gone through as a child, it is up to you to break the cycle of abuse. Break it now, and learn to enjoy your positive future. Misery loves company and you are about to be by yourself, or in jail. What kind of future is that?

You are telling your victims every excuse that you have heard or come up with to make them feel like it's their fault that you assault them. The truth is that it is not their fault. It's yours. No matter what you have seen in your life within your family, no matter what you have had to endure, it is not right that you victimize another human being. Take control back of your life. If you, yourself have been abused, think about what that meant to you and spare someone else that hurt. You will regret it in the end. Get the help you need. Don't be a victim yourself and don't use that as an excuse to victimize anyone else. Do not allow the negatives in your life, become the negatives in another person's life.

Think of everything negative that you have experienced in your life and for every negative thing you have experienced, perform one positive act for someone else. This includes your loved ones that are your victims. They are exactly that, your loved ones. They should be treated as such. You will start seeing the difference within you, as well as the way you interact with your loved ones.

If you need help, for any reason getting help to make a positive change, don't be a coward. Ask for help. The only coward that exist, no matter if you are a man or a woman is the one that doesn't ask for help and make the attempt to change. Take the I initiative and make a positive change in your life. It's ok to let your guard down, because everyone is not out to get you. Don't let people's comments keep you from making the correct choices in life.

If you are the type of person that just does not want to change, I pray for you to see the light and find TRUE happiness in your life. Love yourself and others the way you should be.

Misconceptions men/women use to ok the sexual assault:

- She/he said no but she meant yes
- If she/he gets aroused , she/he must want sex. I just gave her/him what they wanted...Guess what..NOPE
- If she/he didn't want to have sex why did she/he wait so long. It's because they really wanted it
- We have had sex before and she/he never said no

These, among any other excuses you can come up with to justify abusing someone, is never ok. It is never ok to abuse someone, emotionally, sexually, or physically. You must deal with your personal issues that make you abuse. Whether, it's a control issue, insecurities, or other reasons, it's not ok. There is an underlying reason you abuse. You can always try to use the excuse that, you grew up with that. Your father or your mother was the abuser. Do you think you are alone?

There are four groups of people when it comes to abuse. Now this isn't the case with everyone, but most people fall into one of these four categories; People who have been abused themselves in the past, those that have a parent being abused, someone who has witnessed abuse in their family and choose to break the chain of abuse and change their lives, or those that abuse because of their past of being hurt. They develop insecurities and try to use abuse to control their partner, and people who come from non abusive families and for whatever reason, they are abusive. You have the choice to choose how you live your life, and no one deserves to be abused.

Imagine how happy you could be in your relationship if you didn't have to abuse the one you love and use that abuse to FORCE them into loving you. Most people want to be with you because of the real you, not the monster you have become. I have heard people say, well I've been hurt and I would rather keep the next one from hurting me. You shouldn't try to make someone love you. If someone hurts you in anyway, then just let them go. Don't make your future and the people in it, pay for your past. It's not fair to them and it's not fair to you. Don't keep it inside of you. Learn from the experience and move on.

No one has the right to abuse you, and you have no right to abuse anyone else. Remember who you were before you raised you hand or voice to another human being. If you have been around abuse all of your life, make that positive change that you need. If you don't know how to make that change, there are places that you can call or contact for help. Break the cycle. You don't have to live in that vicious cycle. Make the conscious effort to make a positive change to a tragic past. It can be done.

Life isn't so bad on the bright side of life.

Best of luck to you!

Blessings!

Resources

The list of resources included in this book are only a small group of people who work tirelessly and endlessly to bring awareness of abuse to the world. Ten percent of the profits from the sale of each book will be put aside and at the end of every month, will be divided equally and donated to the organizations that contributed to making the writing of this book possible.

- National Sexual Abuse Hotline

1-800-656-HOPE (4673)

- RAINN (Rape, Abuse, Incest National Network)

www.rainn.org

- Love Is Not Abuse

http://www.loveisnotabuse.com

- Do SOMETHING

http://www.dosomething.org

- STAND

http://www.standagainstdv.org

- National Coalition Against Domestic Violence

http://www.ncadv.org

- [Male Survivor](http://www.malesurvivor.org)

www.malesurvivor.org

- [Men Thriving](http://www.menthriving.org)

www.menthriving.org

www.ingramcontent.com/pod-product-compliance
Lightning Source LLC
LaVergne TN
LVHW051520070426
835507LV00023B/3215